PRAISE FOR
THE 1ST EDITION

This is the way every golfer should practice.

Arnold Palmer

An interesting group of practice-tee contests. The idea is to practice with a purpose, which will improve your performance on the course. Good book!

Ross Goodner

Golf Digest Magazine

What a great book! I had always wished that someone would put out something along these lines. Pressure practice sure does work wonders in helping to improve golf skills.

Phillip Mason

Mason's Golf Shop

The Golf Bookshop

George, you've written a damn good book. This is the way to practice golf if you want to be good at it.

Ken Venturi

Professional golfer

Sports commentator

This is a wonderful book. It'll help a lot of golfers.

Patty Sheehan
Professional golfer

This book is a must-read. Thanks for sharing.

Dan Quayle
Former Vice President
of the United States

Pressure Games for Golf *is similar to a pilot's flight simulator. As a pilot would practice certain flying situations without ever leaving the ground, a serious golfer can use these games to rehearse practically every shot he would come across during a round of golf.*

Williams-Grand Canyon News

Outstanding book! I think it'll help a lot of players.

Bernhard Langer

The chapter on learning the rules is well worth the price of this book.

William Battle
USGA president

I promise you, this book will definitely change the way you play golf.

Dan Jenkins
Sportswriter

George, you have an absolutely wonderful book here. This is the book that should be in every golfer's bag.

> *Marion McDougall-Herron*
> *6-time winner of the Pacific*
> *Northwest Golf Association*
> *Championship 1934-48*

This is a cool way to practice. I think you'll be very successful with this book.

> *Mark Long*
> *Yardage Book pioneer*

This is the book you didn't know you needed. Pressure Games for Golf *will definitely improve your game. It truly is a standout among golf books, as there is nothing like it in current golf instruction literature.* Pressure Games *is for all skill levels, beginner to PGA teachers and tour players. We're impressed!*

> *Golf Magazine*

Splendid book, George. You should be very proud.

> *Michael Bonallack*
> *Golf Writers Association of America*

FIRST EDITION
GOLFERS AND TEAMS

GOLFERS	GOLF TEAMS
Arnold Palmer	Otterbein College
Ken Venturi	Columbia University
Pat Summerall	New York University
Karsten Solheim	Pace University
Rocco Mediate	Arizona State University
Tom Watson	Raritan Valley CC
George H.W. Bush	University of Lowell
Dan Quayle	Emerson College
Peter Jacobsen	Tufts University
Nick Price	Stonehill College
Michael Bonallack	CC of Rhode Island
Larry Mize	University of Arizona
Billy Mayfair	University of Maine
Paul Azinger	Northern Maine Tech
Bernhard Langer	Saint Joseph's College
Gary McCord	Providence College
Hubie Green	U of Rhode Island
Payne Stewart	Harvard University
Patty Sheehan	Dartmouth College
Lars Larson	Massachusetts Institute
Ted Shulz	Brown University
Ed Oldfield, Sr.	U of New Hampshire
Gary Wiren	Maine Maritime Academy
Dan Jenkins	Rutgers University-Camden
Alice Cooper	Seton Hall University
Sandra Palmer	Trinity College
Dow Finsterwald	Yale University
	Princeton University
	(and over 300 others)

Book design by Crosstown Typesetting

Cover design by Egypt Rain Designerz

ISBN - Second Edition Paperback : 978-0-945151-01-2

ISBN - Ebook : 978-0-945151-02-9

Second Edition : March 2024

ISBN - First Edition Paperback : 0-945151-00-4
(13-digit converted ISBN - 978-0-945151-00-5)
Out-of-print

Park1000Press
PUBLISHERS

Park1000Press@gmail.com

For
Julie Anne
&
John Nathan

From
Dad

To
Peggy

For
Dr. George & Madeline Dragan

my very first golf teachers,
and my grandparents

And, to
Arnold & Winnie Palmer

And, for
Don O'Hare
Cheyenne Mountain High School
Golf Coach

who taught me my
very first pressure game
in 1969

PRESSURE PRO TIPS...

Gary Player
Pressure is what you make for yourself when you're not prepared.

Tommy Armour
Pressure is a word that is misused in our vocabulary. When you start thinking of *pressure*, it's because you've started to think of failure.

Bobby Jones
Golf is a game that is played on a 5-inch course—the distance between your ears.

Peyton Manning
Pressure is something you feel when you don't know what the hell you're doing.

Lee Trevino
You don't know what *pressure* is until you play for five bucks with only two bucks in your pocket.

Billie Jean King
Winning comes down to who can execute under *pressure*.

Tiger Woods
Pressure causes tension. Relax your muscles before taking that shot.

Sam Snead
Pressure can rush the backswing. Keep it slow and smooth.

Annika Sorenstam
To fight *pressure*, stay committed to your routine before each shot.

Ben Hogan
Placing the ball in the right position for the next shot is 80% of winning.

Walter Hagen
Pressure reveals character. Stay tough mentally when it counts most.

Jack Nicklaus
Commit to your routine fully. Don't just go through the motions.

Payne Stewart
To practice under *pressure* is to play your best on the course.

Arnold Palmer
Success in this game depends less on strength of body than strength of mind and character.

Bobby Knight
The key is not the will to win—everybody has that. It is the will to prepare to win that is important.

C O N T E N T S

PRESSURE GAMES FOR GOLF

INTRODUCTION TO THE 2ND EDITION

First tee —— Your turn to hit—all eyes are on you—you tee up—take your stance—waggle—swing—you hit a beautiful duck hook over the fence and out of bounds—WHAT HAPPENED, you ask yourself?— **PRESSURE.**

18th green —— Your ball is three feet from the cup—all you need to do is sink it for a birdie and you win the match—you line up—take your stance—again, all eyes are on you—you putt—the ball stops three inches short of the hole— WHAT HAPPENED, you ask again?— **PRESSURE.**

There are a thousand situations like these in the game of golf—*pressure situations*—that cause even the best players to choke. Having a 3-foot putt for birdie seems like a simple task until you step up to the ball. Then, this 3-foot putt looks more like a 6-footer aimed at a thimble-sized target. What you are experiencing is nervous tension, or **PRESSURE.**

Top performance under pressure is what ***PRESSURE GAMES FOR GOLF*** is all about. You will experience, on the practice tee and green, almost every shot you might come across during a round of golf.

PRESSURE GAMES FOR GOLF is not an instruction book on grip, stance, or swing. That information can be provided by a PGA professional, through online videos, or one of the many fine golf instruction books available.

This book is meant to be a *practice manual*—a supplement to *any* type of golf instruction you are now receiving. If you are taking lessons three times a week or would just like to try the latest golf tip, ***PRESSURE GAMES FOR GOLF*** will help make your practice time more effective and enjoyable.

CONSISTENCY UNDER PRESSURE

The three words above state the entire philosophy of this book. Performing consistently well at a sport, while in a pressure situation, is something all athletes try to attain—weekend athletes included.

Any golf pro or instruction resource can give you the basics on technique and shot-making. And when golfers take this information to the driving range, they eventually develop *some* consistency.

But what frustrates most players is that when they go out to play 18 holes with their buddies, they can't seem to reproduce the shots they perfectly hit during practice. *And this is especially true in pressure situations.*

PRESSURE GAMES FOR GOLF is a new way to practice.

Actually, it's not that new. It was the first publication from Park1000Press and came out in 1988. That was long before ebooks, before Amazon.com, before our modern-day internet, and has sold well over 25,000 copies. These books went to PGA pros, weekend amateurs, public and private golf courses, golf equipment businesses, and 300+ university golf coaches in the United States and Great Britain. —Not too bad!

(The first four pages of this book lists some of the pros and golf teams that were kind enough to compliment my first edition efforts. Thanks to all.)

Each game has one specific goal: *to expose the golfer to pressure situations while on the practice tee and green.* The more experience a player has in handling different types of problems, the more consistent he becomes on the course.

This same principle is comparable to the *flight simulator* an airplane pilot would use. With this device, a pilot *practices* flying, but never leaves the ground. The flight is *simulated* through computerized animations. With the many hours spent in a simulator, a pilot is better able to handle pressure situations in the air.

This book is your flight simulator for better golf.

Depending on how serious you are about improving your golf game (or any other skill, for that matter), I recommend one outstanding book that defines the practices of winners: Angela Duckworth's classic, **GRIT: THE POWER OF PASSION AND PERSERVERANCE** (published by Scribner, 2016).

Briefly, *and especially in Chapter 7,* she discusses how the experts use *deliberate practice* when working on becoming more skillful at their chosen *passion.* She writes about setting a *stretch goal,* which is focusing and working on a single specific weakness they want to improve, instead of practicing what they're already good at.

So many golfers go to the driving range and mindlessly hit balls with clubs they're comfortable with, and never really work on the weaknesses they have with the other clubs. I *was* guilty of this, hitting *reliable* 7-iron shots, but never working on my *unreliable* 2-iron game—and my score suffered for it.

PRESSURE GAMES FOR GOLF
 is your master guide to *deliberate practice—*
to play your best, most reliable game ever.

My Arnold Palmer Story

Back in 1989, I was at the right place at the right time during The Tradition senior golf tournament being played in Phoenix, Arizona.

As I watched Arnold Palmer putt out for a birdie on the 18th hole, the lady standing next to me seemed very excited to see him. 'A big fan,' I thought.

I told her I wanted to give him a copy of my golf book. She literally grabbed it out of my hand and leafed through it like she was really interested.

Palmer started coming my way, all smiles after that birdie, then he came over to *her* and kissed her on the cheek.

It was then that I realized I was standing next to Winnie Palmer, his wife.

Winnie said, *"This young man has a book for you."*

He skimmed through it with Winnie, then looked up at me and asked, *"Did you write this?"*

I said, *"Yes, I did."*

He then said, *"This is the way every golfer should practice. Thanks."*

All I can say now is— "T*hank you, Arnold.*

My Jack Nicklaus Story

I've seen Jack Nicklaus play in a handful of tournaments; first in Vail, Colorado during a celebrity match with President Gerald Ford, Danny Thomas, Glen Campbell, and others, then later at a few Phoenix Opens.

In 1986, the final year the Open was played at the Phoenix Country Club, I watched him hit balls on the practice range after he finished his round.

He basically put on a masterclass in the art of a perfect practice routine. What you've seen him do on TV with his pre-shot ritual is exactly what he did for *each and every* range ball. Not once did he just drag a ball over and mindlessly hit it.

Then he turns to me and another player and says, "Always aim for a target." That's all he said for the next hour.

So, you'll see that bit of advice throughout this book—

Always Aim For A Target

Thank you, Jack.

(And by the way, just a few months later, he won his final Masters.)

PRESSURE GAMES FOR GOLF

HOW TO PLAY

PRESSURE GAMES

The goal of **PRESSURE GAMES FOR GOLF** is defined in three words:

—CONSISTENCY UNDER PRESSURE—

The games in this book will put a golfer in stressful situations on the practice tee and green, which will then prepare him or her for similar situations on the course. This chapter will explain *how* to manufacture and deal with this *practice pressure*.

There are two ways to play **PRESSURE GAMES:** (1) Competing against yourself, and (2) competing against others. Either way is an effective practice method. The only prerequisite is *your desire* to be the best you can be at playing the game of golf.

PRACTICING BY YOURSELF

Nearly all the games in this book can be played *solo*. The idea is to *out-perform* yourself. If you can consistently beat your previous day's goals on the practice tee, you will eventually beat your competitors on the golf course.

Games for the solo player start with a description of the pressure situation that the golfer must place upon himself. Some games require that you reach a certain level of proficiency before moving on to the next level. Other games ask you to hit your target "a certain number of times *in a row*".

Whatever the situation, you must be willing to play each game to the end and experience the tension that goes along with it.

Don't short-change yourself. You must *feel* the pressure and *play through it* to eventually eliminate it. Like the flight simulator mentioned in the introduction, gaining experience in problem situations helps the pilot calmly and effectively handle most difficulties. The same theory applies to **PRESSURE GAMES** and the golfer—DON'T QUIT!

PRACTICING WITH OTHERS

Practicing with other golfers is the ideal way to play **PRESSURE GAMES.** Not only are you challenged by your partners, but each practice condition also seems more realistic. The motivation to do well increases ten-fold over practicing alone.

The most effective way I have found to produce pressure situations is to wager something of value. For example, if two friends were to play one of the putting games in Chapter 2, they may agree that the *loser* buys drinks at the snack bar.

Here are some other ideas:

Polishing shoes	Caddying 18 holes
Doing yardwork	Wash and wax car
Cleaning golf clubs	Splitting firewood
Painting the house	Bathing the dog
Full tank of gas	Waxing skis
Weekend babysitting	Building a doghouse
Bucket of balls	Greens fees
Clean the garage	Do the laundry
Mop the kitchen floor	Wash the windows
Picking up dog doo-doo	Mow the lawn

The list is virtually endless. It all depends on your imagination and willingness to pay the price if you lose.

For the "high rollers," here are some unusual bets to make and enjoy:

-A dozen new golf balls
-Dinner in the clubhouse
-Paying for concert tickets
-A generous financial reward
-Round-trip airfare to Hawaii
-Paying car insurance for one year
-Jumping, fully dressed, into the club pool
-Weekend use of the loser's home or car
-Free professional services for one week
-New set of golf clubs, golf cart, or shoes
-Tickets to the Super Bowl or World Series
-Strip Golf (the loser or highest score on each hole must remove an article of clothing, down to the underwear only)

Again, the list is endless. Whatever is going to put you in an uncomfortable (and maybe embarrassing) position, *that* is what will work for **PRESSURE GAMES.**

The *scoring systems* are explained for those games in which two or more golfers are competing. Most of the time, emphasis is placed on the lower score winning (much like an actual round of golf).

When two or more players are tied at the end of a game, a *"sudden victory"* play-off hole is selected.

PRESSURE GAMES can also be enjoyed as *match play* competitions—consult the *USGA RULES OF GOLF* for the match play definitions and rules (which can be found for free at **WWW.USGA.ORG**).

THE 100 ZONE

Over 50% of the average golfer's score is made up of strokes taken within 100 yards of the hole. I call this the **100 ZONE.** Nearly all golfers can reach this zone with two good shots. The problem is, many players take another three, four, five or more shots to get the ball into the cup. I believe practice in the **100 ZONE** should be the **#1 priority** among most high-handicappers.

If you glance at the table of contents, you will notice almost half of the **PRESSURE GAMES** are *putting, chipping, and pitching contests*. They are all within the **100 ZONE.** If this is where *your* strokes are wasted, start on these games today.

VARIATIONS

Back to the flight simulator analogy—when pilots train in a simulator, the instructor will occasionally throw in *unexpected* problems. This could be a limited visibility situation, a wind shear emergency, engine failure, or any other mishap that could bring the plane down.

At the end of Chapters 2-7, I have included a list of various conditions to practice under. Wind, light rain, tall grass, and trees are all part of the game. So, why not include them in your practice? Not *all* days on the golf course are perfect. The idea is to make your *rehearsal* on the driving range simulate the *unexpected* conditions on the course.

It's important that you have fun with these games—don't take them too seriously.

Enjoyable practice sessions eventually lead to enjoyable rounds of golf.

And **PRESSURE GAMES** leads to winning!

2

ON THE GREEN

PRESSURE GAMES
FOR THE PUTTER

Because strokes on the putting green make up a major portion of a golfer's score (in most cases, at least half), this is the largest chapter in **PRESSURE GAMES FOR GOLF.** If directions are properly followed for each exercise, you should experience a moderate to high level of tension or pressure, much like you experience during a competitive round of golf.

Remember—play through the pressure.

I learned my first pressure game while playing on my high school golf team. **AROUND THE HOLE**, taught to me by my coach, Don O'Hare, is an excellent way to start a putting program. (The success I had with **AROUND THE HOLE** inspired many of the **PRESSURE GAMES.**)

Once you begin working with these games/exercises, keep one goal in mind: *consistency under pressure.*

AROUND THE HOLE
1 Player

AROUND THE HOLE, in my experience, is the most demanding of all putting games. Not only are you placed under a great deal of *pressure*, but you will also notice a tremendous improvement in concentration.

Find a flat area on the putting green and place four balls around the cup, as shown in this diagram.

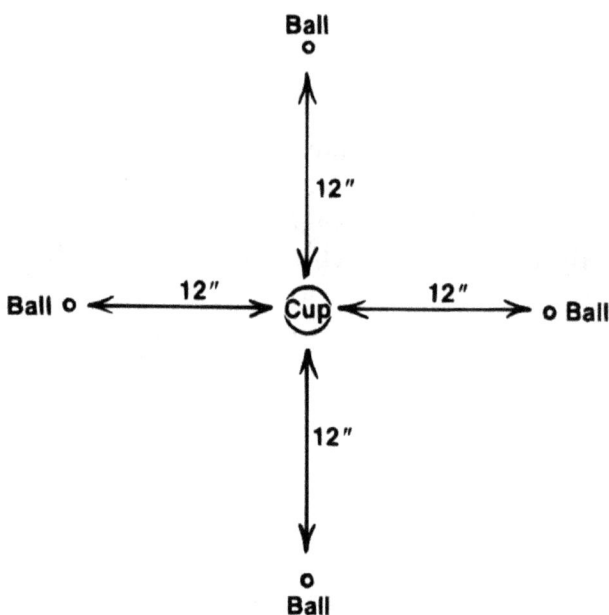

Starting from 12 inches away, putt each ball into the hole. After consecutively sinking all four balls, set them up and do it again.

Your goal is eight perfect putts in a row.

When you reach this goal, move the balls to 1½ feet and repeat the process. Each time, after eight successful shots, increase the distance by 6 inches.

If you miss just *one* putt, go back to the last distance mastered and start over. In other words, you need eight perfect putts before you can advance to the next distance. Miss a putt—go back to the previous distance and try again.

This game can be played at any distance you desire. But the longer the putt, the more difficult it is to sink eight balls in a row.

To develop a dynamic putting game, play **AROUND THE HOLE** to 15 feet. Past 15 feet, try the following goals:

DISTANCE	GOAL
15-20 feet ....ball within 12 inches of hole
20-30 feet ....ball within 18 inches of hole
30 or more feet ....ball within 24 inches of hole

VARIATION— Putt to a tee instead of the cup. *Hitting the tee is the same as sinking the putt.*

VARIATION— Putt on a slightly breaking surface. Arrange the balls so you have one uphill putt, one downhill putt, one breaking left-to-right, and one breaking right-to-left.

18 O'CLOCK
1-4 Players

18 O'CLOCK is a simple 18-hole game that follows the practice green putting clock. No special set-up is needed, but a pre-determined route around the green should be mapped out. Here is one way a 9-hole course could be played.

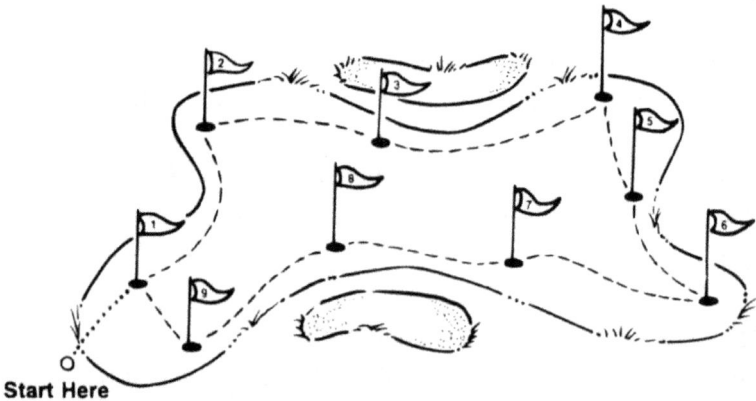

Start Here

If playing by yourself, and using one ball, start near the edge of the green, and putt to Hole 1, *(See illustration)*. Each hole is a par 2, making par for an 18-hole game 36 strokes. If, after 18 holes, your score is over 36, start over at hole 1 and play another round of 18 holes.

Your goal is even par or under.

Keep a record chart of your lowest scores and use your lowest score as a goal for each time you play.

When playing against your friends, simply keep score as you would out on the golf course. *The lowest 18-hole score wins.*

VARIATION— Instead of using the holes, set up 9 or 18 tees on the green and putt to those. *Hitting the tee is sinking the putt.*

Putting is like wisdom: partly a natural gift and partly the accumulation of experience.
—Arnold Palmer

TEE TREE
1-4 Players

TEE TREE can be played solo or with a few friends. It is an excellent way to acquire that special "touch" for distance. To start, set up six tees at various distances from a *common point* on the green. *(See illustration)*

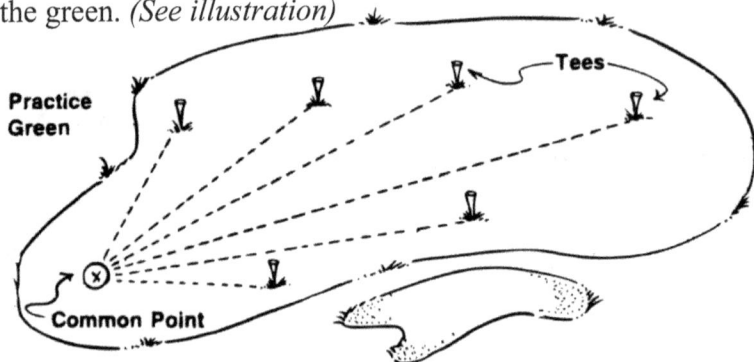

NOTE—*Keep all tees to within 15 feet of the common point.*

If playing by yourself, start with six balls and putt one ball from the *common point* to each of the six tees.

Your goal is to be within 12 inches of each target.

If you reach six targets *in a row*, move your *common point* back 1 foot and continue the game. When a target is missed by more than 12 inches, collect the balls and try again.

Involving two or more players in this game requires a special scoring system. Hitting the tee is 1 point. The players within the target area get 2 points. Missing the target area gets 3 points.

After an "18-tee" match, the lowest score wins

VARIATION— Instead of tees, use the practice-green holes.

TROUBLE PUTT
1 Player

Almost every golfer has a certain putt he or she fears. It could be the left-to-right breaking putt from 4 feet; maybe it's the downhill putt from 8 feet. Whatever type of shot creates tension in your game *can be conquered.*

Before you allow yourself to go home, set up your "trouble putt" using four balls. And don't forget—set up the balls at the distance you need to work on.

Your goal is to hole 5 shots, but not consecutively.

After you become more confident with this shot, increase your level of pressure using the chart below:

LEVEL	GOAL
1	sink 5 out of 20 balls
2	" 8 " 20 "
3	" 12 " 20 "
4.............................	" 15 " 20 "
--	
5.............................	sink 10 in a row
6	" 12 " "
7.............................	" 15 " "
8	" 20 " "

NOTE—*Use this chart for putts no longer than 15 feet. Repeat each level until mastered.*

6 INCHES
1 Player

I'm sure you've heard the phrase "never up, never in." Well, this game will get you up, if not in, nearly every time.

To set up, place a dime on the green. Now, 6 inches beyond the dime, plant a tee. *(See illustration)*

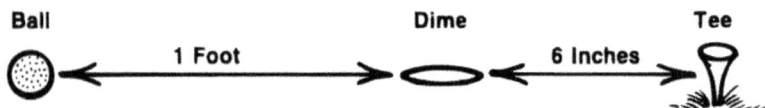

Ball   **Dime**   **Tee**

⟵ 1 Foot ⟶   ⟵ 6 Inches ⟶

Making believe the dime is a cup, your goal is to putt over the dime and hit the tee.

Start putting from 1 foot away. Increase the distance by 6 inches after you have hit the tee eight times in a row. If you miss the tee or come up short, go back to the last distance mastered and start again.

If you really feel motivated, try to work up to 10 feet.

NOTE—*Set this game up on as level an area as possible. You can also set up for **straight** uphill and downhill putts. BUT, avoid using sidehill breaks with a planted tee. Use a regular hole as your target.*

Half of golf is fun—
the other half is putting.

—Peter Dobereiner

CLIMB THE STAIRS
1-4 Players

If you have trouble judging the distance *and* break of a putt, this game may help. **CLIMB THE STAIRS** can be played alone or with friends. It's easy to set up, provided your practice green has a slope to it.

To set up a left-to-right game, place five golf clubs parallel to one another, forming a set of stairs. The clubs should be 8 inches apart. *(See illustration)*

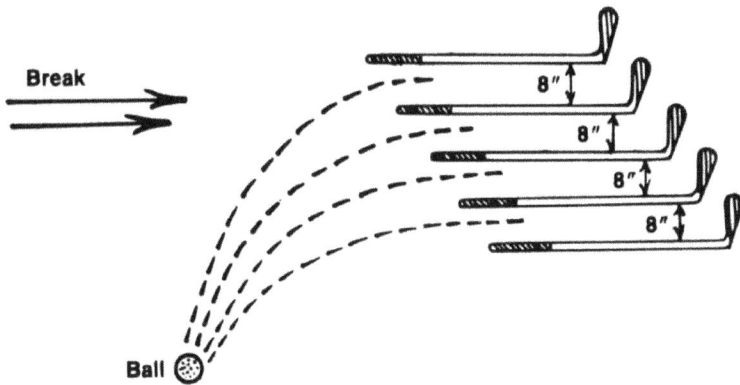

Your goal is to consecutively putt four balls into each opening, using the left-to-right break of the green.

Start with the bottom opening and work your way to the top. If you miss an opening or use a club as a *backstop,* you must go back to the last opening mastered.

Once you have mastered the top opening, you can do one or a combination of the following variations: *increase the distance of the putt; increase the required number of balls; or add more stairs.*

CLIMB THE STAIRS can be turned into a simple putting contest using the following scoring system:

> Player hits the opening = **1 point**
>
> Player misses the opening or uses the club
>
>   as a *backstop* = **2 points**
>
> Player comes up short = **3 points**

The lowest score after 18 putts wins

A good player who is a great putter is a match for any golfer. A great hitter who cannot putt is a match for no one.

—*Ben Sayers*

PUTT 21
2-4 Players

If you remember your high school basketball days, you and some teammates often squared off in a game of *21* to pass the time. Well, adapting this basketball classic to golf is no problem. No special set-up is needed—just a few willing participants and a worthwhile wager.

How To Play PUTT 21

1. Decide on the wager. *(See Chapter 1 for ideas)*
2. Decide who shoots first, second, third, etc.
3. The first player selects the target hole, then putts. The player must putt until the ball is in the hole.
4. All other players take a turn shooting to the same hole and holing out.

Keeping score

1 putt = **3 points**

2 putts = **1 point**

3+ putts = **0 points**

5. Now, player two selects the next hole, and the game continues.

The first player to score 21 or more points wins.

PRO SIDE STRAIGHT
1-4 Players

When Arnold Palmer was winning everything but the Irish Sweepstakes back in the late 50s and early 60s, there was one thing he did on the green that emphasized the difference between professionals and amateurs; Palmer almost always "charged" the hole. He putted the ball hard enough so that if he ever missed, the ball would go *beyond* the hole, and not be left short.

Just think back over your last few rounds of golf—how many strokes could you have saved if only the ball would have gone another 2 inches?

PRO SIDE STRAIGHT is similar to the game **6 INCHES,** but with one difference—this time, you get to shoot at the cup. To set up, plant one tee about 12 inches beyond the target hole. For now, it is important that you set up on a flat section of the putting green—no sidehill, uphill, or downhill putts.
(See illustration)

Ball	Direction of Putt	Hole		Tee

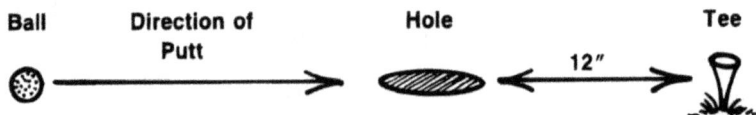

Start putting with four balls from 3 feet away, stroking the ball firmly enough to reach the tee. If your putt is on line, the *hole* will get in the way.

You should remember that your target is the tee, not the hole.

Sink eight balls consecutively from 3 feet, then increase the distance by 1 foot. *(See the following goal chart.)*

DISTANCE	GOAL
3 feet	sink 8 in a row
4 feet.................................	" 8 " "
5 feet.................................	" 8 " "
6 feet	sink 8 out of 10
7 feet	" 8 " 10
8 feet	" 8 " 12
9 feet	" 8 " 12
10 feet	" 8 " 15

$\boxed{\textit{VERY IMPORTANT RULE}}$ — If you miss a shot and are past the hole, start over from that same distance. **BUT, if you ever come up short of the hole, <u>start over from 3 feet</u>.** I know this sounds harsh, but the end result will be well-worth the effort.

When competing with a friend or two, try the following scoring system:

One holed putt = **1 point**	
Beyond the cup within 12 inches = **2 points**	
Beyond the cup more than 12 inches = **3 points**	
Short of the cup = **4 points**	

Lowest score for 18 holes wins

PRO SIDE BREAKING
1-4 Players

Watch the pros during any given tour event on TV and you will notice one important thing—whenever they miss a breaking putt, they almost always miss on the *high side* of the hole. This *high side* is also known as the **pro side.**

Most amateurs, when missing a breaking putt, will send their ball to the *low side,* or **amateur side,** of the cup. So, let's eliminate that unprofessional habit today.

For **PRO SIDE BREAKING,** find a hole on the practice green that breaks **left to right.** Next, place a tee 2 inches to the left of the hole. *(See illustration)*

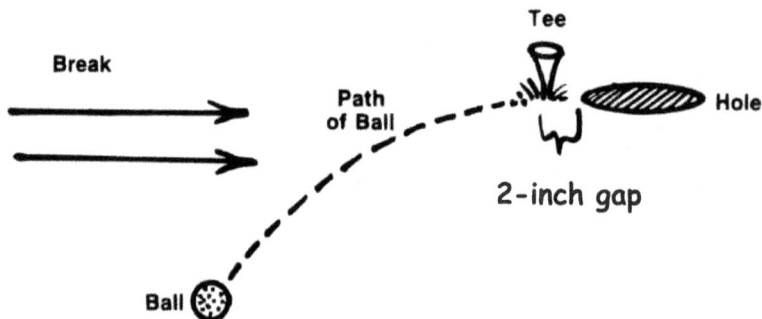

Putting from 3 feet, your goal is to sink the ball. If you miss, you should miss through that 2-inch gap between the tee and the hole, and nowhere else. This is called missing on the **pro side.** The principle is the same as **PRO SIDE STRAIGHT**—you should give the ball a chance to drop. These "chances" will pay off more times than you think.

Your goal from 3 feet is to sink eight putts in a row. When mastered, move to 4 feet, and sink eight more.

If you miss on the *pro side* <u>within</u> the 2-inch gap, start over from the same distance.

BUT, if you miss on the *amateur side,* (the <u>low side</u> of the hole), **start over at 3 feet**.

Use the chart to adjust your **PRO SIDE BREAKING** target, according to the length of your putt:

PUTT LENGTH	TARGET SIZE	GOAL
3 feet .... 2-inch gap.......................	sink 8 in a row
4 feet.......... 2 " "....................	" 8 " "
5 feet...........3 " "......................	" 8 " "
6 feet .... 3 " "......................	sink 8 out of 10
7 feet .... 3 " "......................	" 8 " 10
8 feet .... 4 " "......................	" 8 " 12
9 feet .... 4 " "......................	" 8 " 12
10 feet .... 4 " "......................	" 8 " 15

To play against your friends, score as follows:

Sinking a putt = **1 point**

Missing on *pro side* = **2 points**

Missing on *amateur side* (or <u>above</u> *pro side)* = **3 points**

Short of the hole = **4 points**

Lowest score for 18 holes wins

TEE LINE TOUCH
1-2 Players

When it comes to putting, always remember that distance is *slightly* more important than direction. This is certainly true on those long 30 and 40-footers. Stopping the ball hole-high, or a bit past the hole, on a 35-foot downhill putt will surely eliminate some unnecessary strokes. **TEE LINE TOUCH** is a great way to develop a feel for distance.

First, set up six tees in a straight line on the green as shown in the illustration, and setting the tees 2 feet apart:

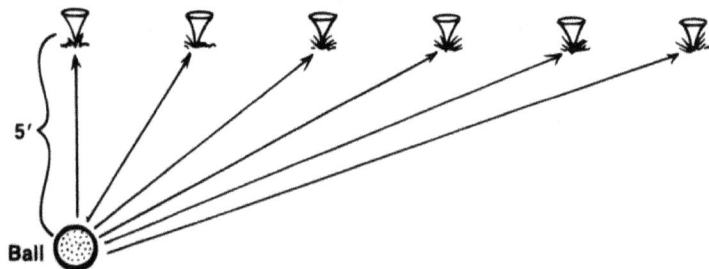

To play, putt one ball to each tee. You will notice that with each consecutive target, the distance increases.

> *Your goal is to hit or go past the tee*
> *and avoid coming up short.*

Play **TEE LINE TOUCH** until you can putt to all six tees without coming up short, for four consecutive times. If you miss just one shot, start over at tee number one.

Try this game with a friend using this scoring system:

Hitting the tee = **1 point**
Past the tee = **2 points**
Short of the tee = **3 points**

Lowest "18-tee" score wins.

TEE CUP
1-4 Players

TEE CUP is a game encouraging you to hit *past* the hole. More putts will drop when they are hit firmly enough to travel beyond the target.

To set up, plant a pair of tees on the green, leaving a 4¼ -inch gap between them *(4¼ inches is the diameter of a regulation cup).*

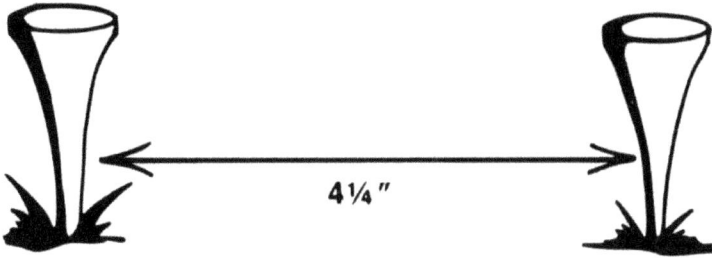

4¼ "

Start from 3 feet away and putt eight balls *through* this gap. If you miss one or come up short, start over.

After eight consecutive shots through the gap, go to 4 feet and repeat the process. If you miss a shot, go back to the last distance mastered and start again.

For a little competition with your buddies, score this game as follows:

Through the tees = **1 point**
Outside the tees = **2 points**
Short of the tees = **3 points**

Lowest score after 18 holes wins.

DUEL
2 Players

In **DUEL**, two players square off at opposite holes and "shoot it out" with one another.

What really makes this game interesting is the *size of the wager*. For the youngsters, a Coke at the snack bar is usually enough. But, for you "high rollers, try a dozen new Titlest golf balls, a new putter, or maybe the use of your Porsche for the weekend. In other words, make it worthwhile.

To begin, players stand about 15 feet apart, each next to a hole on the practice green. Using two balls on each turn, the first player putts to the other player's hole, and scores as follows:

(refer to illustration below for description of *the leather*)

Sinking the putt = **1 point**

Ball stops within *the leather* of opponent's putter = **2 points**

Any putt on or outside *the leather* = **3 points**

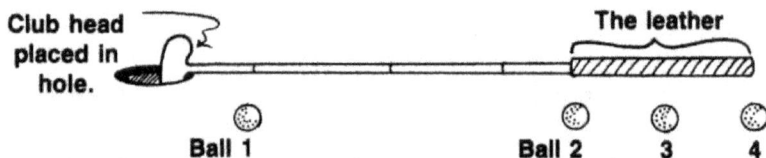

In the illustration, balls 1 and 2 are considered *within the leather*, and balls 3 and 4 are *on the leather*. (In all fairness, only one designated putter should be used as the measuring tool. The distance from clubhead to *the leather* varies among putters.)

After the first player putts and scores two balls, the second player does the same. The first player with 30 points or more is eliminated. BUT, if Player 1 reaches 30 points and Player 2, on their next turn, also reaches 30 or more points, consider this a tie, and play a new game.

There is no similarity between golf and putting—they are two different games. One is played in the air, and the other on the ground.

—Ben Hogan

HORSE PUTT
2 Players

This game is played like the favorite classic basketball game, **H-O-R-S-E**. It requires two players, a worthwhile wager, and a little putting creativity.

To start, Player 1 chooses a hole and putts to it. If he sinks the shot, Player 2 must make the same shot, or be given the letter **H**.

If Player 1 misses, Player 2 then selects the next hole.

The Player reaching H-O-R-S-E first, loses

VARIATION— *example*: Player 1 goes for a long putt and misses but decides to keep putting until the ball is IN the hole (let's say it took two putts).

Now, Player 2 must sink the same putt in two shots. If he fails, he receives a letter.

BUT, if he sinks the ball with *one putt*, Player 1 can try to make the putt in one shot or receive a letter.

VARIATION— Instead of using **H-O-R-S-E**, try other golf-related words, such as:
- **P-U-T-T-E-R**
- **N-I-C-K-L-A-U-S**
- **F-L-A-G-S-T-I-C-K**
- **H-O-L-E-I-N-O-N-E**
- **D-O-U-B-L-E-B-O-G-E-Y**

ON THE GREEN VARIATIONS

Being an experienced golfer, you know that variety makes the game more interesting. And, not every golf course situation is identical to the perfect environment on the practice range.

Below is listed a few of these situations which you can apply to some of the putting games:

Putt from the fringe or a sand trap.

Putt during extreme weather conditions—wind, rain, heat, cold.

Putt on a wet green, or an extremely dry green.

Visit other golf courses to experience different types of greens and grasses.

Try a putting tournament with your friends. Select four different **ON THE GREEN** games with the winner of each game competing in a final fifth game.

Create your own variations. You never know what your situation will be on the golf course.

A GOOD IDEA

If you have a problem with consistently leaving your putts short of the hole, try putting with plastic practice balls.

Use the balls that have the holes in them and, using a pencil, stuff the balls with torn up cotton rags. This gives the balls some weight, so it feels like you are really *hitting* something solid.

You will find that you need a firmer stroke to send the ball to the cup, and this *feel* will carry over to when real golf balls are used.

Putts get real difficult the day they hand out the money.

—Lee Trevino

3

SHORT SHOTS

PRESSURE GAMES
FOR PITCHING AND CHIPPING

This chapter on **SHORT SHOTS** will help develop the chipping and pitching part of your game. There are many exercises in this section, all simulating common playing situations faced on the course.

Practice these games as presented, and *DON'T LOOK FOR THE EASY WAY OUT.*

But, above all— *have fun with them.*

AROUND THE CLOCK
1-4 Players

AROUND THE CLOCK is a great competitive game for 2, 3, or 4 players. *(Single-player directions are below.)*

To start, designate a spot to chip from about 5 feet off the edge of the green. *(See diagram).*

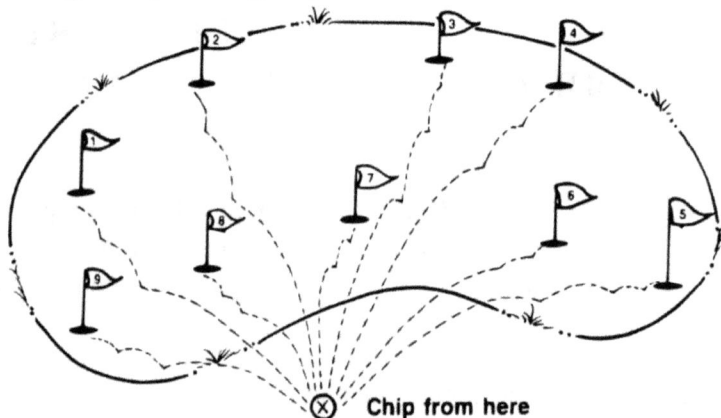

Chip from here

Each player is allowed one ball and their favorite chipping club. Next, everyone chips to the first hole on the putting clock.

Score as follows:

Sink your chip = **1 point**
Within the leather = **2 points**
    (See **DUEL** in Chapter 2 for the
        definition of "the leather")
Outside the leather = **3 points**
	**Lowest score after
	18 holes wins.**

If you wish to play by yourself, try the following game:

Set up 5 feet from the edge as described prior, but use eight balls instead of one. The target will be a 2-foot diameter circle surrounding the cup.

Your goal is to put all eight balls into this 2-foot circle before advancing to the next hole.

Stay on the same hole until you successfully make eight chips <u>in</u> <u>a row</u>.

This may sound difficult for the high-handicapper, but it can be done. In fact, mastering just one hole will probably cut 2-3 strokes off your game.

NOTE— *If you want more of a challenge, reduce the size of the target circle. And/or, increase the distance from the green.*

This is a game of misses. The guy who misses best is going to win.
—Ben Hogan

CLIMB THE STAIRS
1-4 Players

If you have been through the putting section of *PRESSURE GAMES FOR GOLF*, you are already familiar with **CLIMB THE STAIRS**. This is a great game to develop the "touch" for distance and the "know-how" for breaking chips.

To set up a left-to-right breaking game, find a sloped area of the practice green and place five golf clubs parallel, as shown below: Set the clubs 12 inches apart, forming a set of stairs as in the

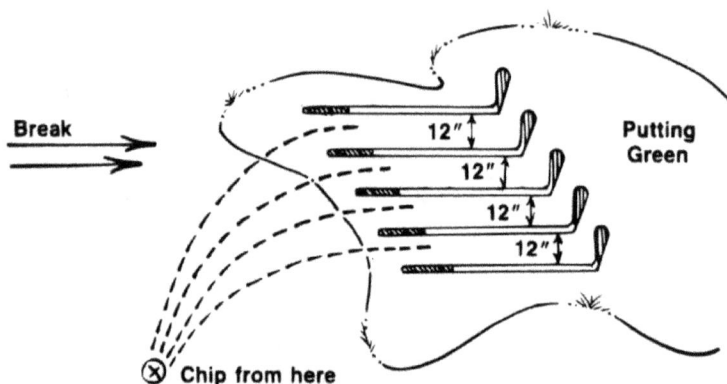

Break →

12"

12"

12"

12"

Putting Green

⊗ Chip from here

illustration. Your chipping spot should be about 5 feet off the green. (You can also set up the clubs in the opposite way for right-to-left breaks.)

> *Your goal is to consecutively chip four balls into each opening, using the left-to-right break of the green.*

Start with the bottom opening and work your way to the top. Each chip must *roll* into the open slots, not fly in.

If you miss an opening, go back to the last one mastered and start over. Once you reach the top level, increase the distance, increase the number of balls, or add more stairs.

If you play **CLIMB THE STAIRS** with your friends, use one ball each.

Use the following scoring system:

Player hits the opening = **1 point** Player over-shoots the opening = **2 points** Player comes up short = **3 points**	**Lowest score after 18 chips wins.**

Pressure is what you live for—if you're going to be successful in life, you're going to have pressure.

—Jack Nicklaus

CHIP AND A PUTT
1-4 Players

Chipping your ball to within one-putt range is a tremendous stroke saver, and especially if you do it 8-10 times over 18 holes. **CHIP AND PUTT** will help develop the consistency a proficient golfer needs.

To start, place four balls off the edge of the green, about 5 feet from the fringe. (*See diagram*)

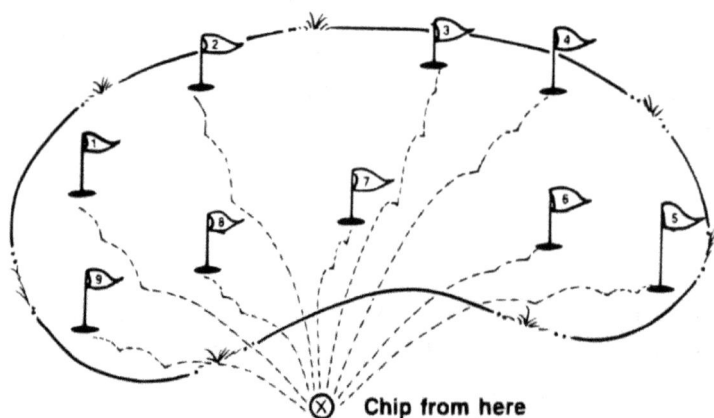

Chip from here

Your goal is to chip each ball to within one-putt range of the hole, and finish the shot using your putter.

In other words, you are allowed a chip and a putt to sink your ball. If you miss a shot, start over on that same hole until mastered. BUT, to increase the pressure, when a shot is missed, start over on hole number one.

To play competitively, set up 5 feet off the green with each player using one ball. Simply keep score as you would during a round of golf.

Low score after 18 holes wins

HORSE CHIPS
2 Players

Playing **HORSE CHIPS** is very similar to **HORSE PUTT** in Chapter 2. Instead of sinking your chip, aim for a general target area around the hole. In this case, the target size depends on how far off the green you are.

Use the chart below to determine the target diameter:

DISTANCE FROM GREEN	TARGET DIAMETER
5 feet	2 feet
6-10 "	3 "
11-15 "	4 "
16-20 "	5 "
21-25 "	6 "

To play the game, first determine how far off the green you will chip from, then select the target diameter.

Next, Player 1 chips to any hole he wishes. If his ball is within the target, or he sinks his chip, Player 2 must only land in the target area. If Player 2 misses, he receives an **H**.

But, if the player selecting the target *misses* the announced target, his turn is skipped and the next player selects a target.

If Player 2 <u>makes</u> the shot, he selects the next hole.

The Player reaching H-O-R-S-E first, loses

In this game, *closest to the hole* does not count. Your ball only needs to be within the target diameter.

NOTE— After you have mastered the 21–25-foot range, go back to the top of the chart and change **DISTANCE FROM THE GREEN** and **TARGET DIAMETER** to <u>yards</u>:

(For example, a distance of 5 feet is now 5 yards, and the target goes from 2 feet to 2 yards.)

VARIATION— Instead of using **H-O-R-S-E**, try other golf-related words, such as:
- **G-R-E-E-N**
- **G-O-L-F-C-A-R-T**
- **M-U-L-L-I-G-A-N**
- **O-U-T-O-F-B-O-U-N-D-S**
- **P-E-N-A-L-T-Y-S-T-R-O-K-E**

VARIATION— Recalling the basketball game **H-O-R-S-E**, and with a little creative thinking, you can add more players to this game.

I don't fear failure, but I fear not trying.
—Tiger Woods

CHIP TO TEE
1-4 Players

CHIP TO TEE is a game that will enhance a golfer's ability around the green. Once mastered, though, the pay-off is truly remarkable.

Start by placing two tees on the putting green, 4¼ inches apart, and about 5 yards from the edge of the green. Next, pick a chipping spot 5-7 feet off the green. *(See illustration)*

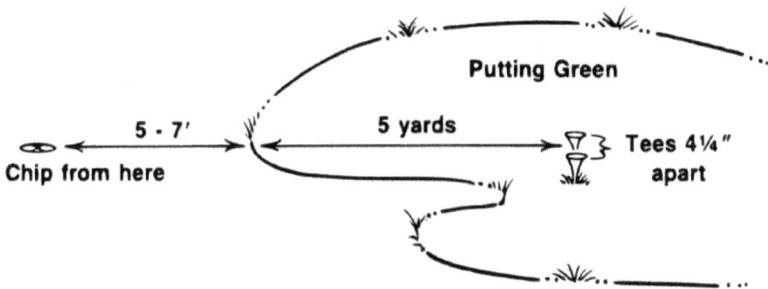

Your goal is to chip through the 4¼-inch opening, and not go more than 3 feet past.

NOTE— If a ball touches a tee while going through the target, count this as a successful shot. Later, when you get better at this game, adopt the rule of touching a tee equals a missed shot.

Work your way up to 20 consecutive shots using the following schedule:

LEVEL	BALLS THROUGH THE TARGET
1	2 out of 20 shots
2	5 " "
3 ....….................	8 " "
4	10 " "
5	4 in a row
6	8 "
7	10 "
8	15 "
9	20 "

Any ball that goes through the target, and is more than 3 feet past the tees, does not count. Stay on each level until mastered.

If you wish to *increase the pressure,* whenever a shot is missed, go back one level.

To challenge your friends, try this scoring system:

Through the target and within 3 feet = **1 point**

Through the target and past 3 feet = **2 points**

Wide of target = **3 points**

Short of the target = **4 points**

After 18 chips, the lowest score wins

Good luck with this one!

WAGON WHEEL
1 Player

WAGON WHEEL is a variation of the earlier chipping game, **AROUND THE CLOCK,** but was developed strictly for a single player. It's simple, yet demanding, and can almost guarantee to get you up and down in two strokes or less.

On the practice green, plant eight tees around a hole, making a 2-foot diameter circle. *(See diagram)*

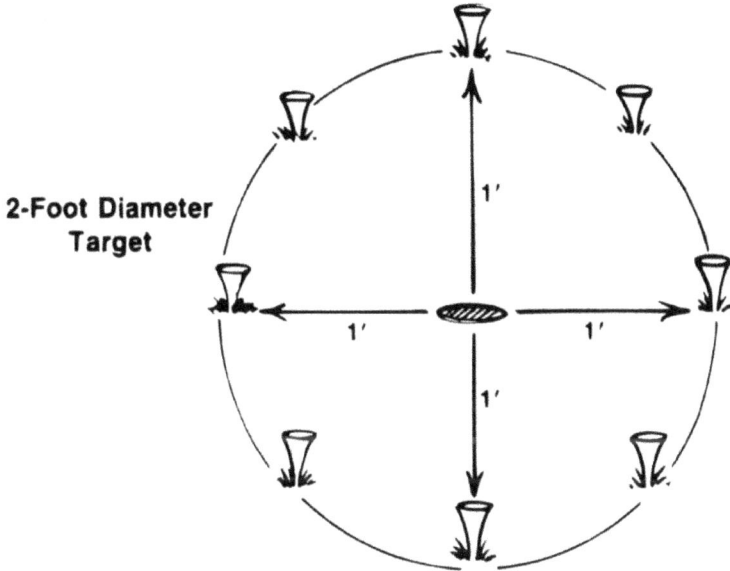

2-Foot Diameter Target

1' 1' 1' 1'

Starting 5 feet off the green, chip 20 balls, attempting to stop each within the target circle.

Work your way up to 20 successful target shots *in a row* using the following schedule:

LEVEL	TARGET SHOTS
1	2 out of 20 balls
2	5 " "
3	8 " "
4	10 " "
5	4 in a row
6	8 "
7	10 "
8	15 "
9	20 "

If you miss a shot, start over at the same level. But, to add a little more pressure, go back one level when a shot is missed.

After mastering Level 9, move the chipping spot 10 feet from the green and start over on Level 1. *Do not increase the target size.*

Again, when Level 9 is conquered from 10 feet, add another 5 feet, and start over.

If you think you are beaten—you are.
—Walter Hagen

ON THE FLY
1-4 Players

In order for your ball to land somewhere near the cup, it must first hit the green *on the proper spot.*

For this game, we are not concerned with how close to the cup the ball is. Here, we are sending our chip *on the fly* to a square target on the green. The ball must hit this target first before rolling to the hole.

There are two ways to set up the target:

Use four tees to form an 8-inch square on the green. *(See diagram)*

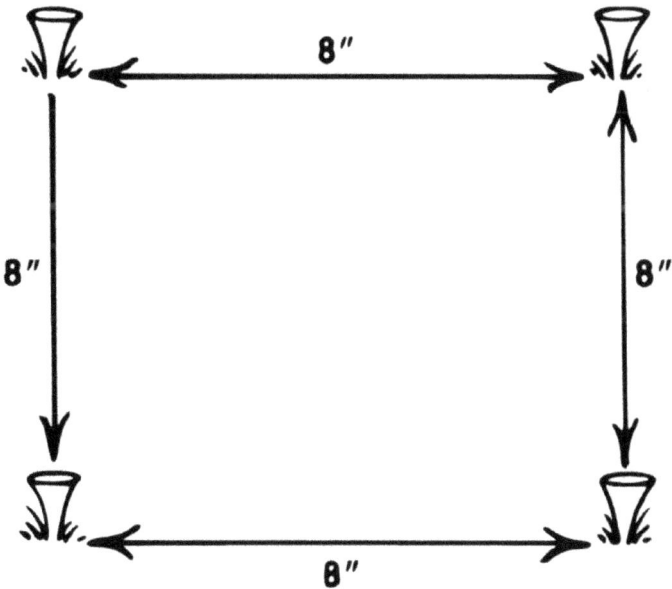

Or, using a couple of tees, anchor two score cards to the green. *(See diagram)*

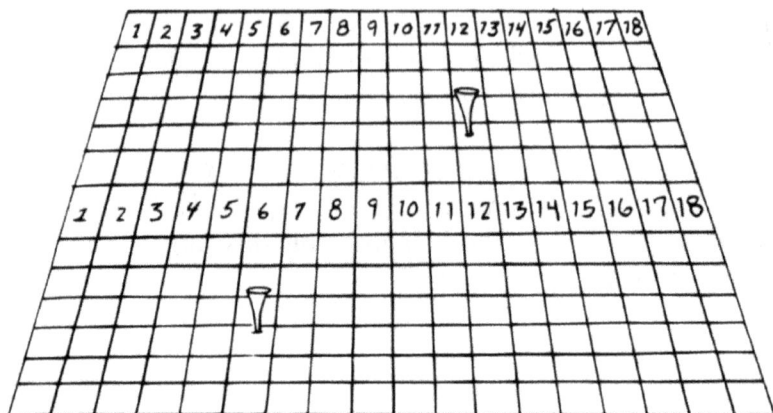

The scorecards work best for two reasons— you can *see* your target, and you can *hear* the ball hit.

The single player's <u>goal</u> is to land five consecutive chips on the target. As you get better, increase this number to 8, 12, 15, then 20 in a row. If you miss a shot, start over.

Playing with your "betting" friends, score your game as follows:

> Hit the target <u>on the fly</u> = **1 point**
> Miss the target = **2 points**

30 or more points eliminates a player. The last player left wins.

NOTE— ON THE FLY is best played *within 10 yards of the green.*

UP AND OVER
1-4 Players

UP AND OVER is a game that helps reduce the pressure one feels when trying to chip *over* an obstacle. Small bushes, sand traps, grass mounds, and water are just a few of the problems every golfer must face during any 18-hole round.

UP AND OVER is a "2 in 1" game— not only must you chip over an obstacle, you must hit a target upon landing.

The best way to set up is, first, find an obstacle to hit over. Let's use a sand trap for this example. Next, place 20 balls at about 5 feet from the trap. Your target will be a 2-foot square mapped out by planting four tees on the green. *(See diagram)*

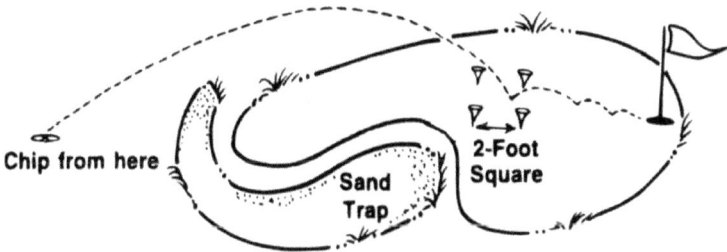

Chip from here

2-Foot Square

Sand Trap

Your goal is to land the ball, on the fly, inside the 2-foot square.

Don't be concerned where the ball ends up, just concentrate on hitting the target.

Work your way up to 20 "direct hits" in a row using the following schedule:

If you miss a shot, start over on the same level.

LEVEL	TARGET SHOTS
1	2 out of 20 balls
2	5 " "
3	8 " "
4	10 " "

5	4 in a row
6	8 "
7	10 "
8	15 "
9	20 "

NOTE—UP AND OVER can be played in the backyard of your home. In place of a sand trap, use some stacked tires, a large plastic sheet, or a doghouse *(minus the dog)*. The target can be a sheet of newspaper, a rolled-up garden hose, or whatever you think you can hit. *Be creative.*

To play against your friends, try this scoring system:

Up and over with a direct hit = **1 point**
Up and over, missed the target = **2 points**
Hitting, or being short of the obstacle = **3 points**

Decide on how many "holes" to play (usually 18) with the winner having the lowest score

HIGH LOB
1-4 Players

There are occasions when a high lob shot (or flop shot) close to the green is necessary. And, there are three basic reasons to use this shot: first, you may have to clear a tall obstacle between you and the green, like a bush or a small tree, or second, you need to stop the ball very quickly before it rolls way past the cup. The third reason would be a combination of these two situations.

Tom Watson, Tiger Woods, and especially Phil Mickelson, are masters of this shot. Do a YouTube search for these three golfers and you'll see what I mean.

HIGH LOB is much like the game **UP AND OVER**—you must *lob* your ball over an obstacle and hit a designated target on the green. If done correctly, the ball will have minimum roll after it lands. Ideally, it will roll no more than two feet.

The best way to set up is, first, find an obstacle to hit over. Since you're practicing on a driving range, a tall obstacle to lob over may not be readily available. So, as in **UP AND OVER**, let's use the sand trap and a little imagination.

NOTE— You could prop up your golf bag about six feet in front of your ball and use that as your obstacle.

So, let's pretend you're hitting over a bush that is close to the green. Next, place 20 balls about 5 feet from the *bush*. Your target will be a 2-foot square mapped out by planting four tees on the green. *(See diagram and goal chart, which are the same set-ups from* **UP AND OVER***)*

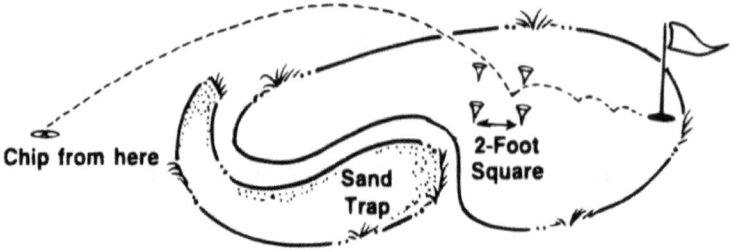

Your goal is to land the ball, on the fly, inside the 2-foot square.

Don't be concerned where the ball ends up, just concentrate on hitting the target. Work your way up to 20 "direct hits" in a row using the following schedule:

LEVEL	TARGET SHOTS
1	2 out of 20 balls
2	5 " "
3	8 " "
4	10 " "
5	4 in a row
6	8 "
7	10 "
8	15 "
9	20 "

If you miss a shot, start over on the same level.

NOTE—HIGH LOB can be played in the backyard of your home. In place of a sand trap, use some stacked tires, a large garbage can, a kid's swing set, or a doghouse *(minus the dog)*. The target can be a sheet of newspaper, a rolled-up garden hose, a beach towel, or whatever you think you can hit. *Be creative.*

To play against your friends, try this scoring system:

Up and over with a direct hit =	**1 point**
Up and over, missed the target =	**2 points**
Hitting, or being short of the obstacle =	**3 points**

Decide on how many "holes" to play (usually 18) with the winner having the lowest score

Golf is assuredly a mystifying game. It would seem that if a person has hit a golf ball correctly a thousand times, he should be able to duplicate the performance at will.

—Bobby Jones

BANK SHOT
1-4 Players

A bank shot does not come up too often during a round of golf, but when it does, proper execution can save you two strokes each time. All this game requires is a grass-covered mound and 20 practice balls.

Set your chipping spot about 5 yards from the mound. Next, and 5 yards on the other side of the mound, set up a target; your golf bag is an excellent target for this game. *(See diagram)*

Your goal is to play a "bank shot" off the mound and land near the target.

Even more challenging, land the ball *on* the target <u>after one bounce</u>. The following chart will assist you in mastering this game:

LEVEL	TARGET SHOTS
1	4 out of 20 balls
2	6 " "
3	8 " "
4	10 " "

If you miss a shot, start over on the same level.

NOTE— Since ground conditions are impossible to control, our chart will only go through four levels.

As a competitive game, **BANK SHOT** can be scored as follows:

> Hitting the target = **1 point**
>
> Missing the target = **2 points**
>
> Short, or completely over the mound = **3 points**

Lowest score after 18 chips wins

VARIATION— Instead of shooting to a target *past* the mound, set up a 2-foot square target <u>on the mound</u>. Use four tees to construct your target square. Your chip should hit this square and bounce over the mound. If you wish, set up a target on the other side, as well.

Golf can be best defined as an endless series of tragedies obscured by the occasional miracle.

—Unknown

DON'T GO HOME YET
1 Player

Before quitting for the day, try this game— it's simple, yet frustrating, but well worth the time:

Pick a spot 5-15 feet off the edge of the green. Next, lay down 20 balls and start chipping to any one hole.

Your goal is to sink five chips, <u>not consecutively,</u> before going home.

The better you get at this game, the higher your goal should be.

For beginners, start on a fairly flat section of the putting green. Then, as you improve, you should start adding some break to the green.

The thing to remember is *never give up.* The pay-off will appear on your scorecard.

VARIATION— What kind of chip are you having trouble with? The one from high grass? The left-to-right break? Chipping off of hardpan?

Whatever your problem, place 20 balls in that particular situation and chip away. Again, don't go home until you sink at least five balls.

NOTE— In these games, don't try to sink five chips in a row, or five out of 20. The magic number is 5, no matter how many balls you shoot.

BACKYARD GOLF
1-4 Players

As stated earlier, accurate chipping can shave many unnecessary strokes off your game. Spending at least 50% of your practice time on the short game would definitely *not* be overdoing it.

When you can't get out to the practice range or golf course, try **BACKYARD GOLF.** Set up a 9-hole chipping course in your backyard, complete with obstacles and targets.

You might try the following 9-hole set-up:

HOLE	OBSTACLE	TARGET
1 —	5' x 5' plastic sheet	— Old towel
2 —	Lawn chair	— Clothes basket
3 —	Barbecue grill	— Sheet of newspaper
4 —	Cardboard box	— Plastic hoop
5 —	Stacked tires	— Rolled-up hose
6 —	Doghouse	— Old blanket
7 —	Bushes or hedge	— Cardboard box
8 —	Picnic bench	— Old shirt
9 —	Small wading pool	— Bicycle tire

Each hole should be about 15-25 feet in length, consist of an obstacle and a target, and have a par of 1. To par a hole, a player must chip *over* the obstacle and land, *on the fly,* on the target. Making the ball stay *within the target* is unnecessary.

Keep score as you would a regular round of golf, or match play. The winner "supervises" the Saturday afternoon yardwork.

SHORT SHOTS VARIATIONS

Many of the **SHORT SHOTS** games can be played with these variations:

- Chip from different lies— Hardpan, loose dirt, sand, rough, tall grass, wet grass, uphill, downhill, sidehill, under a bush or tree, restricted backswing, next to a rock, from a divot, etc.

- Chip to a sloped green.

- Chip to a wet or very dry green.

- Extreme conditions— Wind, heat, cold, rain _with no lightning_, noise, talking, traffic sounds.

- Visit other golf courses to experience different types of greens, grasses, and environments.

- Create your own variations— you never know what type of situation you will encounter on the course.

A GOOD IDEA

If you want to hit full-swing shots, but don't quite have the available space, try using plastic practice balls. Use the balls that have the holes in them, and, using a pencil, stuff the balls with torn up cotton rags. This gives the balls some weight, so it feels like you are really _hitting_ something solid.

4

MADE OF IRON

PRESSURE GAMES
FOR THE IRONS

Back in the late 1960s, statistics were compiled on some of the world's top golfers from 1960 to 1968. The top four players (Arnold Palmer, Jack Nicklaus, Gary Player, and Billy Casper) were compared.

Results showed Nicklaus had the worst driving and putting records of the four. So, how did he win 30+ tournaments, including seven majors?

He hit over 75% of the greens with his approach shots, as compared to 67% for his three fellow competitors. Even by today's standards, Jack Nicklaus would still be in the top position for 2024.

I use this story to illustrate one thing: *hitting the green in regulation can save you a bunch of strokes.* Your goal, for nearly every iron shot, is to land the ball <u>on the green</u>.

SOLO 7
1 Player

Consistently well-struck irons are a major key to success in golf.
SOLO 7 will help develop that consistency and help you deal
with the pressure of hitting the target in crucial situations.

On the practice range, start with the pitching wedge.

Your goal is to land seven consecutive shots
on a specific target.

If you miss a shot, start over. Hitting a target seven times in a row
may sound difficult at first, but starting with the pitching wedge
and working your way up through the 2-iron is the surest way to
master each club.

So, where's the pressure?

Well, if you have been hitting a 6-iron on the range all afternoon,
and you finally hit the target six times in a row, you will definitely
feel the pressure on that 7th shot. Because, if you miss, you have
to start over.

Target size is not as important for **SOLO 7** as it is for the putting
and chipping games. You are shooting for a general area, with
each target increasing in size as you play the short irons through
the long irons.

Try the following target size comparisons with the corresponding clubs:

CLUB	TARGET SIZE COMPARISON
PW - 8-iron	8 - 15 feet diameter (small swimming pool)
7 - 5-iron	15 - 30 feet diameter (large car, small green)
4 - 2-iron	30 - 50 feet diameter (large swimming pool, medium-size green)

If you would like a more specific target, aim for a sprinkler head, a flagstick, a clump of grass, or a bare spot that is *within* the target.

Although you may be spending a great deal of time on this game, the pay-off will be extraordinary. Just look at Jack Nicklaus!

Concentration comes out of a combination of confidence and hunger.
—Arnold Palmer

DISTRACTION
1-4 Players

At least once during a round of golf, a player is faced with the following situation:

Their ball is sitting near a small plant, an out-of-bounds stake, or a fence post. When the golfer takes a practice swing, he sees this obstruction out of the corner of his eye and makes some unnecessary mental adjustments.

He may say to himself, "I know I'm going to hit that stake," or "maybe if I swing real hard, I'll chop right through that clump of weeds."

Thoughts like these will ruin a golf swing and obviously ruin your chance for a par.

The game **DISTRACTION** was developed to help you handle *distracting* situations.

Simply place an object on the ground very close to your ball. The object should be _at least one CLUBHEAD LENGTH_ from the ball, but no closer.

Items that make great distractions include:

Piece of crumbled paper
Another golf ball
Pine cone/leaves
A pile of tees
Scorecard
Paper cup
Soda can
Golf bag

You are to play the ball as it lies, shooting at a specific target, and all while attempting to block out the distraction.

Your goal is to hit the target seven consecutive times.

What you are doing here is getting used to playing your ball from a tight situation. Swing freely without altering the clubhead path. Ninety-nine percent of the time, the obstruction will never come into play.

Try playing **DISTRACTION** with a few brave friends. Pick the target — set up the obstruction — and shoot away.

Score as follows:

Hitting the target =	**1 point**
Missing the target =	**2 points**
Hitting the obstruction =	**3 points**

After 18 shots, the lowest score wins

The secret of golf is to turn three shots into two.

—*Bobby Jones*

HIT AND RUN
1-4 Players

The game **HIT AND RUN** is a little shot that comes in handy when you find yourself under a tree or shooting into a strong wind. The ball is hit low and rolls quite far after landing. The well-rounded golfer should know how to play this shot, and especially in a pressure situation.

About 50 yards out on the range, choose a 20-foot diameter target spot.

Your goal is to play hit-and-run shots, landing seven consecutive shots on the target, and <u>on the fly</u>.

After hitting the target, the ball will roll. *Keep in mind (or write it down) how far the ball rolls with each club.*

Start with the 8-iron and work through the 2-iron. You must hit the target spot seven times in a row before advancing to the next club. Each successful hit must be made with a *low trajectory* hit-and-run shot. If you miss the target, start over.

For some friendly competition, try this scoring system:

Hitting the target with a hit-and-run shot = **1 point**

Missing the target with a hit-and-run shot = **2 points**

Hitting anything *other than* a hit-and-run shot = **3 points**

After 18 shots, the lowest score wins

NOTE— Each player may use a favorite club for this game.

THE SLOPE
1-4 Players

When you watch the pros on television, notice that almost all of them land their approach shots in the same general area on a sloped green. The reason for this is landing in the correct area makes putting much easier. For instance, an uphill putt is far easier than a downhill putt.

So, when hitting to a green, make sure you aim for the slope *below* the hole.

This **PRESSURE GAME** needs a sloped putting green-type target, like you would find at most driving ranges.

Your goal is to put seven balls, in a row, on this sloped target, and on a specific area below an imaginary hole.

Before you shoot, decide where on the green the imaginary pin is located. If the pin is in the right back corner, your target should be the right side of the green, and *below* the hole. If successful, this approach shot would set up an uphill putt.

Start with the pitching wedge (or sand wedge) and work your way up to the 2 or 3-iron. If you miss a shot, start over with that same club.

As a competitive game, **THE SLOPE** can be scored as follows:

Landing on the specific target = **1 point**

Landing somewhere on the green = **2 points**

Missing the green entirely = **3 points**

After 18 shots, the lowest score wins

IRON HORSE
2-4 Players

IRON HORSE is a competitive game requiring proper target selection and an accurate iron shot. It is played much the same way as **HORSE CHIPS** in the previous chapter.

Player 1 selects and shoots to a target. If his ball hits the *announced target,* Player 2 must hit the target. If Player 2 misses, he gets an **H.** The next player, then selects the next target.

But, if the player selecting the target *misses* the announced target, his turn is skipped and the next player selects a target.

Each golfer who accumulates the letters H-O-R-S-E is eliminated, and the last remaining player wins.

VARIATION— Instead of using **H-O-R-S-E**, try other golf-related words, such as:
- **G-R-I-P**
- **D-I-V-O-T**
- **S-W-I-N-G**
- **S-T-A-N-C-E**
- **H-A-N-D-I-C-A-P**
- **W-O-R-M-B-U-R-N-E-R**

VARIATION— To make the game more challenging, select the *route* your ball must take to the target. For example, announce that the target is the 150-yard sign, and it must be approached with a *hook.* Or tell your partners that the shot is a *hit-and-run* at the 100-yard marker. Just be creative.

IN A ROW
1-4 Players

IN A ROW, like all **PRESSURE GAMES,** is a simple game that builds your consistency while under pressure.

Your goal is to hit, <u>in a row</u>, as many balls as you can onto a target. Then, each consecutive day, beat yesterday's record by at <u>least one</u> shot.

For example, on Monday, you land three 8-iron shots <u>in a row</u> on your target. Then on Tuesday, your goal is to land at least four 8-irons, <u>in a row</u>, on the target. The objective is to beat your previous record.

Start with a sand wedge or pitching wedge— once your "all-time record" achieves 20 or more successful shots on the target, go to the next club. Work your way through the 2-iron.

Use the chart below to determine the target diameter:

CLUB	TARGET SIZE
PW - 8-iron	8 - 15 feet in diameter
7 - 5-iron	15 - 30 " " "
4 - 2-iron	30 - 50 " " "

Although you can play **IN A ROW** by yourself, it is a lot more fun to compete with your friends.

To play with your buddies, first agree on a target. Player 1 shoots to the target using any iron he chooses. If he makes the shot, he gets one point and keeps shooting until he misses. Player 2 then does the same.

The object is to hit the target as many times <u>in a row</u> as you can, collecting one point for each success

20 points is a game, but depending on your skill, this number can be adjusted higher or lower.

VARIATION— Require that each shot fades or draws to the target. Also, try high and low shots, hit-and-run shots, or any other creative ways to approach a target.

Pressure is self-induced. Pressure is affected by fear. Be bold—attack the pin.
—Arnold Palmer

LESS THAN FULL
1-4 Players

Once in a while, you may need to play a 70-yard 6-iron over a pond, a 100-yard 2-iron into the wind, or an easy pitching wedge to a tight pin placement. A **PRESSURE GAME** built around these "less than full" shots can be extremely helpful to the serious golfer.

To start **LESS THAN FULL**, choose a 20-foot diameter target, 60 yards out on the driving range.

Your goal is to land seven consecutive shots on this area.

Repeat the process with each club, going from a pitching wedge or sand wedge, and working through a 2-iron. Once you master a club, move to the next one— if you miss a shot, start over with that club.

After the 60-yard range is conquered, shoot to a spot 70 yards away, going from a pitching wedge through a 2-iron. Once mastered, increase the distance by another 10 yards.

REMEMBER— your target diameter will stay at 20 feet. If the increased distance is difficult to hit, just increase the size of the target to 30 – 40 feet. But, to achieve pro-status and increase the pressure, keep it at 20 feet.

NOTE— After a certain distance, some clubs will be eliminated. Refer to the chart: >>>

TARGET DISTANCE	CLUBS TO USE
60 yards	PW – 2-iron
70 "	PW – 2-iron
80 "	PW – 2-iron
90 "	PW – 2-iron
100 "	PW – 2-iron
110 "	9-iron – 2-iron
120 "	8-iron – 2-iron
130 "	7-iron – 2-iron
140 "	6-iron – 2-iron
150 "	5-iron – 2-iron
160 "	4-iron – 2-iron
170 "	3-iron – 2-iron

To play against your friends, score as follows:

Hitting the target on the fly = **1 point**

Missing or short of the target = **2 points**

Landing on the fly *over* the target = **3 points**

Low score after 18 shots, wins

If profanity had any influence on the flight of the ball, the game of golf would be played far better than it is.

—*Horace G. Hutchinson*

NO BACKSWING
1-4 Players

Occasionally, you may come across a shot where your backswing is severely limited. Your ball might be right next to a tree, an embedded rock, or some other natural obstacle where free relief is not allowed. **NO BACKSWING** is the perfect practice game to prepare you for this type of situation.

This is an iron game because using a wood to get out of trouble is basically asking for more trouble. An iron is easier to control and much more responsive to "muscling" out of a tight spot.

To set up, either find an area on the range; maybe next to a garbage can, a tree trunk, over-hanging branches, or some other obstruction where your backswing is restricted.

You can also manufacture this problem by placing your golf bag, cart, or a chair behind your ball, or hitting from under a sign.

The obstacle needs to be close enough to where you can't take a full backswing.

Next, throw some balls down and, with your abbreviated swing, try to hit a target out on the range. Don't make the target area too far away since you won't be making a full swing at the ball.

The object is to hit your ball out of trouble and onto a nearby target.

To compete with yourself, your *beginning goal* is to hit your target five times in a row. If you miss, start over.

Your ultimate goal is to hit your target 10 times in a row.

If you reach your goal, change the obstacle to something different. For example, if your first obstacle is a tree trunk, and you successfully hit 10 shots in a row to the target, switch to some low-hanging branches and start over.

The more varied your obstacles are, the more prepared you become when on the course.

If competing with friends, each player gets one shot before the next player shoots.

Score as outlined below:

> Hitting the target = **1 point**
> Missing the target = **2 points**
> Short of target = **3 points**

Lowest score after 18 shots wins

VARIATION— Decide what club can be used. All players must use a 7-iron, or a 3-iron, etc.

NOTE— Whatever kind of shot that gets you out of trouble is the *correct shot.* It doesn't have to look *pretty,* as long as it gets you to your selected target. Remember what Ben Hogan said: "Your goal is to win, not to show off."

ONE-ARMED BANDIT
1-4 Players

Once in a blue moon, you may not be able to address the ball as you would a normal shot. This would happen if you were too close to a tree, a cactus, the edge of a pond, immediately next to a sand trap, or next to a large, embedded rock.

In situations like these, sometimes your only option, besides a penalty stroke for moving the ball, is to hit it using one arm—be it your left arm or your right arm.

Again, like the Pressure Game **NO BACKSWING,** this is an iron game. Trying to save yourself with a wood might not be worth the potential trouble. You *can* practice with your woods in this game, but trying to hit a decent shot *consistently* is difficult.

To set up, find an area on the range; maybe next to a garbage can, a tee marker, or a tree trunk; or use your golf bag, a chair, a golf cart, or a range-ball basket.

Next, set a ball, either on the right side or left side of the obstacle, and set up for hitting it out onto the range toward a *nearby* target.

Use your imagination here and pretend you can only hit the ball with one arm—a full swing with both arms and the proper stance is impossible, okay?

Now, *facing the driving range,* if you're practicing with your right arm, place the ball on the right side of the obstacle. Next, with your *back toward the range* and using an iron, swing your right arm up and back to hit the ball toward your target. Use a 5, 6, or 7-iron for this shot.

This type of shot is going to need a lot of practice before it feels comfortable, but once you master it, you'll look like a golfing genius.

Remember, select a target area close to you. Hitting a ball backwards with one arm will not travel as far as a full-swing shot.

The object is to hit your ball out of trouble and onto a nearby target.

To compete with yourself, your *beginning goal* is to hit your target five times in a row. If you miss, start over.

Your ultimate goal is to hit your target 10 times in a row.

If competing with friends, each player gets one shot before the next player shoots.

Score as outlined below:

Hitting the target = **1 point**
Missing the target = **2 points**
Short of target = **3 points**

Lowest score after 18 shots wins

VARIATION— Decide what club can be used. All players must use a 7-iron, or a 5-iron, etc.

And I'll again channel the great Ben Hogan:

"Your goal is to win, not to show off."

MADE OF IRON VARIATIONS

Several of the **MADE OF IRON** games can be played with the following variations:

- Shoot from various lies— Hardpan, loose dirt, sand, rough, tall grass, wet grass, uphill, downhill, sidehill, under a bush or tree, restricted backswing, next to a rock, from a divot, etc.

- Extreme conditions— Wind, heat, cold, rain _with no lightning_, noise, talking, traffic sounds.

- Require that your shot fades, draws, slices, hooks, flies high, runs low, or a combination of these.

- Try hitting next to a fence, a large rock, or any other distraction you can think of.

- Shoot from a tee instead of off the ground.

- Try swinging from the other side (i.e. if you play right-handed, rotate the clubface and swing left-handed).

- Try hitting the ball with your back to the target and swinging with one hand.

- Visit other golf courses to experience different types of greens, grasses, and environments.

If you play on a course where tree-trouble is common, try some of these **MADE OF IRON** games while shooting *out of the woods:*

Set up about 10 yards into the woods, find an opening through the trees, and shoot away *toward your target.*

Also, place yourself in the situations you sometimes face when playing your home course. Practice these shots over and over, aiming for and maybe hitting your target.

Remember, your goal is to get out of the woods and land somewhere close to your selected target.

After practicing these trouble shots over and over, you will definitely feel more confident when a problem arises.

NOTE— Shooting out of the woods at Latrobe Country Club was how Arnold Palmer practiced golf as a kid.

A GOOD IDEA

If you want to hit full-swing shots, but don't quite have the available space, try using plastic practice balls. Use the balls that have the holes in them, and, using a pencil, stuff the balls with torn up cotton rags. This gives the balls some weight, so it feels like you are really *hitting* something solid.

5

IN THE WOODS

PRESSURE GAMES
FOR THE FAIRWAY WOODS

Hitting the fairway woods is probably the least threatening of all golf shots. With the three, four, and five woods, contacting the ball to produce a fairly respectable shot is not that difficult.

A fairway wood, with its rounded bottom and curved face, tends to push the grass aside and not dig into the turf as an iron does. A more detailed explanation of the fairway wood advantage can be found in any complete instruction manual, or from your PGA professional.

By observing amateur golfers for many years, I found the fairway woods to be the least-used clubs in the bag. It is for this reason that there are only a few games discussed in this chapter. These **PRESSURE GAMES** will give you the experience you need to handle a majority of situations that come up.

SOLO 7
1-4 Players

Like **SOLO 7** for the irons, this same game can be used with the fairway woods. Again, the one difference is the increased target size. **SOLO 7** will help develop consistency and help deal with the pressure of hitting the target in crucial situations.

On the practice range, and starting with the 5-wood, your goal is to land seven consecutive shots on a specific target.

If you miss one, start over. After mastering the 5-wood, move on to the 4-wood, then the 3-wood. If you're wondering where the pressure comes in, wait until you hit six perfect shots in a row— that seventh shot is going to feel like the deciding stroke to beat Jack Nicklaus at the Masters.

Target size should be about the same for all fairway woods. Aim for an area the size of a small green (10-20 yards wide). If you want a more specific target, aim for a bare spot, a flagstick, or a yardage marker within the target area.

Spend your time wisely on this game. *Shoot for a target, not for distance.* To repeat what Ben Hogan said: "Your goal is to win, not to show off."

To play competitively with your buddies, score as follows:

Landing and staying on the target <u>on the fly or a roll</u> = **1 point**
Missing or short of the target = **2 points**
Landing over the target = **3 points**

Low score after 18 shots, wins

IN A ROW
1-4 Players

If you have played through the iron games, you are already familiar with **IN A ROW.** The one difference here is the increased target size. Because of the great distance involved, there is a larger margin for error. Therefore, your target should be about 10 to 20 yards wide.

If you wish to play on your own, simply hit as many balls as you can to a specific target.

If, on one day, your record is five consecutive target shots at the 200-yard marker, the next practice session should require at least six shots in a row on the target before going home.

Your goal is to break the previous day's record, eventually reaching 20 target shots.

Begin with the 5-wood. Once you reach 20 or more consecutive target shots, go to the 4-wood and repeat. Then the 3-wood.

To play with your friends, first select a target about 200 yards out. Next, Player 1 shoots to the target using any fairway wood he wishes. If he makes the shot, he gets one point and keeps shooting until he misses.

Player 2 then does the same. The object is to hit the target as many times in a row as you can, collecting one point for each success. The first player to reach 20 points wins, but depending on your skill, this number can be adjusted higher or lower.

WOODEN HORSE
2-4 Players

WOODEN HORSE is a competitive game requiring proper target selection and an accurate fairway wood shot. It is played much the same way as **IRON HORSE** in Chapter 4, but the target size and distance are increased.

Player 1 selects and shoots to a target (at least 160 yards away with a target 10-20 yards wide). If his ball hits the *announced target,* Player 2 must hit the target. If Player 2 misses, he gets an **H.** The next player then selects a new target.

But, if the player selecting the target *misses* the announced target, his turn is skipped and the next player selects a target.

Each golfer who accumulates the letters H-O-R-S-E is eliminated, and the last remaining player wins.

VARIATION— Instead of using **H-O-R-S-E**, try other golf-related words, such as:
- **S-L-I-C-E**
- **S-H-A-N-K**
- **C-L-U-B-F-A-C-E**
- **R-U-L-E-B-O-O-K**
- **S-C-O-R-E-C-A-R-D**
- **C-O-M-P-E-T-I-T-O-R**

VARIATION— To make the game more challenging, select the *route* your ball must take to the target. For example, announce that the target is the 200-yard sign, and it must be approached with a *hook.* Or tell your partners that the shot is a *hit-and-run* at the 200-yard marker. Just be creative.

IN THE WOODS VARIATIONS

Several of the **IN THE WOODS** games can be played with the following variations:

- Shoot from various lies— Hardpan, loose dirt, sand, rough, tall grass, wet grass, uphill, downhill, sidehill, under a bush or tree, restricted backswing, from a divot, etc.

- Extreme conditions— Wind, heat, cold, rain _with no lightning_, noise, talking, traffic sounds.

- Require that your shot fades, draws, slices, hooks, flies high, runs low, or a combination of these.

- Try hitting next to a fence, a large rock, or any other distraction you can think of.

- Shoot from a tee instead of off the ground.

- Visit other golf courses to experience different types of greens, grasses, and environments.

- Try using your driver as a fairway wood, but only if the ball is sitting up nicely on the grass.

The best wood in most amateurs' bags is the pencil.

—Chi Chi Rodriguez

If you play on a course where tree-trouble is common, try some of the **IN THE WOODS** games while shooting *out of the woods.*

NOTE— Don't try to be a hero and make the green your target, especially if it's 200 yards away. A ball ricocheting off a 50-year-old oak tree at 100+ mph would make a sizeable dent in your forehead.

- Set up about 10 yards into the woods, find an opening through the trees, and shoot *toward your target.*

- Place yourself in the situations you sometimes face when playing your home course. Practice these shots over and over, aiming for and maybe hitting your target.

Remember, your goal is to get out of the woods and land somewhere close to your selected target.

After practicing these trouble shots over and over, you will definitely feel more confident when a problem arises.

A GOOD IDEA

If you want to hit full-swing shots, but don't quite have the available space, try using plastic practice balls. Use the balls that have the holes in them, and, using a pencil, stuff the balls with torn up cotton rags. This gives the balls some weight, so it feels like you are really *hitting* something solid.

6

DRIVE

PRESSURE GAMES
FOR THE DRIVER

Let's face it— you're on the first tee, the guys watching through the window in the clubhouse see you teeing up your ball, your playing partners are watching and evaluating your pre-shot routine, your waggle, your stance, your outfit, your shoes, your cool sunglasses. The little golfer in your brain is telling you, "Don't slice it, don't top it, don't whiff it, left arm straight, yada-bing-bang-boom."

Finally, you take the club back, all goes silent, you swing— a beautiful worm-burner, right down the middle and within 20 yards of where you were just standing. —Dead silence—

In my opinion, the drive is the most important, yet, most pressure-producing shot in golf. Hitting a great drive, and especially off the first tee, does three things:

1) It puts your ball in perfect position for the approach shot.
2) It puts you in a totally confident, almost fearless, practically undefeatable state of mind.
3) It puts pressure on your opponent (unless he's also a student of *PRESSURE GAMES FOR GOLF*).

PRESSURE GAMES FOR GOLF

The games and variations included in this chapter will take you through most tee-off situations with the driver or fairway woods.

Remember, your goal is to be consistent
while under pressure

EDUCATED CURVE
Pre-game Preparation

If your normal tendency is to slice or hook your drives, it would be to your advantage to *educate* that curve. Knowing in advance how far to the right your slice will travel, or how far to the left your hook will take you, has its benefits.

Jack Nicklaus played a natural left-to-right fade on his drives, and he knew how many yards to the left he had to aim to eventually hit his target. He was quoted as saying, "The hardest shot in golf is a *straight* drive."

Your goal is to find out how many yards to the left or right your drive travels.

First, hit 40-50 balls, aiming directly at a specific point 250 yards out. After hitting each ball, make a note as to how far (estimating) left or right of the target the ball landed.

After 50-100 shots, you should have a pretty good idea where you need to aim to compensate for your natural curve.

NOTE— As your game improves over the next weeks and months, you will need to repeat this measurement process several times.

Although **EDUCATED CURVE** is not an actual **PRESSURE GAME,** use the information gathered to play the remaining **DRIVE** games.

The woods are full of long drivers.

—Harvey Penick

85

LOW BRIDGE
1-4 Players

Shooting into the wind or below a line of trees requires a special shot—*the low drive.* This is a great shot to use on the windy British, Texas, and Florida courses. Basically, it is nothing more than a very long hit-and-run shot. The following **PRESSURE GAME** will help you develop this shot.

On the practice range, select a spot to shoot from that requires a low drive. Next to a line of trees is ideal. If this type of set-up is not available, just try to keep the ball *low.*

Next, select a target about 200-250 yards out. The target should be about the size of a small green (10-15 yards wide).

Your goal is to shoot seven consecutive low drives at the target.

If you miss or shoot too high, start over.

To play this game with your friends, try the following system:

Hitting the target with a low drive = **1 point**
Hitting the target with a regular drive = **2 points**
Missing the target either way = **3 points**

Lowest score after 18 drives, wins

VARIATION— For a more realistic situation, play this game on a windy day.

NOTE— Try to develop a *draw* on this shot. The counter-clockwise spin on the ball bores through the wind better and will roll much further than a fade or a straight drive.

SOLO 7
1 Player

SOLO 7 is a single-player game that develops consistently accurate drives when under pressure. Because of the great distance involved (240-280 yards), your target size will be very large (15-30 yards wide).

Using your driver, the object is to land seven consecutive shots on a specific target.

If you miss one, start over.

Again, the target should be the size of a large green. Then, the more accurate you become, the smaller the target should be. If you can't hit seven target shots in a row, start with three and work your way up gradually.

I think most pros would agree: the drive is the most important shot in golf. When it comes to driving the ball, accuracy is much more important than distance.

Spend your time on **SOLO 7** developing accuracy—the distance will come later.

VARIATION— To make **SOLO 7** more challenging, attempt to hit your target with a fade or draw.

Golf is an awkward set of bodily contortions designed to produce a graceful result.
—Tommy Armour

CLOSE CALL
1-4 Players

Once in a while, a golfer must position his drive near a bunker, pond, tree, or stream, making his approach shot much easier. **CLOSE CALL** develops this skill and helps you realize the importance of drive placement strategy.

Setting up this game is simple. Find a suitable target about 200-260 yards out on the range. This could be a yardage marker, dirt mound, flagstick, tree, water sprinkler, etc.

Your goal is to shoot seven consecutive shots slightly to the left or right of the target, but not actually land on the target.

For example, the 200-yard marker could represent a sand trap on the left side of the fairway. The object is to place your drive to the right of the *imaginary sand trap,* putting it in perfect position for a clear shot to the green. *If you miss, start over.*

When you practice by yourself, choose a target, and try shooting to the left or right of it, successfully hitting the ideal landing area seven times in a row. If you land "in the hazard," start over.

To play with friends, score as follows:

Landing in the ideal area = **1 point**

Landing too far from the *hazard* = **2 points**

Landing in the *hazard* = **3 points**

Lowest score after 18 drives wins

VARIATION— Select two *imaginary hazards* and try to land the ball between them.

JUST PASSING BY
1-4 Players

How close can you come to a tree or a fence without hitting it? Sometimes, to place your drive in an ideal position on the fairway, you need to tee off where you will come dangerously close to a line of trees, maybe a water tower, or possibly a small building. **JUST PASSING BY** will help eliminate some of the pressure and fear of going for that ultimate drive placement.

To start, find a place on the practice range that requires you to shoot extremely close to a fence or tree. These spots are found on the left and right sides of the range. If you want to practice a fade, shoot from the left side of the range and away from the tree/fence. To practice a draw, shoot from the right side.

Your goal is to hit a selected target seven consecutive times.

The catch is you must come within 5 yards of the fence or tree while the ball is in the air. This is extremely difficult, but well worth the practice.

To play competitively, score as outlined below:

Missing the trees/fence by about 5 yards and hitting the target area = **1 point**

Missing the trees/fence <u>by more than</u> 5 yards and hitting the target area = **2 points**

Missing the target = **3 points**

Hitting the trees/fence = **4 points**

Lowest score after 18 drives wins

HORSE DRIVER
2-4 Players

If you have gone through **PRESSURE GAMES,** you will recognize this one. **HORSE DRIVER** is just another variation of the basketball game **H-O-R-S-E.** I feel it offers variety and challenge for the serious player, as well as putting him in a pressure situation.

Using a driver, Player 1 selects, announces, and shoots to a target (that's at least 200 yards away). If he hits the target, Player 2 must do the same. If Player 2 misses, he gets an **H,** and the next player selects a new target.

But, if the player selecting the target *misses* the announced target, his turn is skipped and the next player selects a target.

Each golfer who accumulates the letters H-O-R-S-E is eliminated, and the last remaining player wins.

Your target should be about the size of a large green (or smaller, if all players agree).

VARIATION— Instead of the letters **H-O-R-S-E,** try these other golf-related terms:
- **L-I-N-K-S**
- **D-O-G-L-E-G**
- **B-A-C-K-S-P-I-N**
- **A-P-P-R-O-A-C-H**
- **B-U-M-P-A-N-D-R-U-N**

VARIATION— To make the game more challenging, select the *route* your ball must take to the target. For example, announce that the target is the 250-yard sign, and it must be approached with a *draw* or a low wind-cheater bump-and-run. Be as creative as you can with the driver.

IN A ROW
1-4 Players

IN A ROW, like the iron and fairway-wood versions, is an excellent game for developing tee-shot consistency under pressure. This version is played with the driver or 3-wood.

If you wish to play on your own, simply hit as many balls as you can to a specific target.

If on one day you hit your 250-yard target four times in a row, the next day's goal should be at least five consecutive shots.

Your goal is to break the previous day's record, eventually reaching 15 target shots.

To play with friends, first select a target about 250 yards out. Next, Player 1 shoots to the target using a 3-wood or driver. If he makes the shot, he gets one point and keeps shooting until he misses. Player 2 then does the same.

The object is to hit the target as many times *in a row* as you can, collecting one point for each success. The first player to reach 20 points wins. But, depending on your skill, this number can be adjusted higher or lower.

VARIATION— require that each shot fade or draw. Also, try low and high shots.

NOTE— Your target should be 15-30 yards wide, about the size of a large green.

DRIVE VARIATIONS

To add a little more challenge to the **DRIVE GAMES,** try the following variations:

- Instead of using a driver or 3-wood, try the other fairway woods off the tee.

- Extreme conditions— Wind, heat, cold, rain _with no lightning_, noise, talking, traffic sounds.

- Require that your shot fades, draws, slices, hooks, flies high, runs low, or a combination of these.

A GOOD IDEA

If you want to hit full-swing shots, but don't quite have the available space, try using plastic practice balls. Use the balls that have the holes in them, and using a pencil, stuff the balls with torn up cotton rags. This gives the balls some weight, so it feels like you are really hitting something _solid._

What other people find in poetry or art museums, I find in the flight of a good drive.
—Arnold Palmer

7

ON THE BEACH

PRESSURE GAMES
IN THE SAND

Next to the water hazard, the greenside bunker is the most feared animal on the golf course. This fear sprouts mostly from the golfer's lack of knowledge on how to hit out of a sand trap.

ON THE BEACH will *not* explain the stance, grip, or swing technique for escaping the sand. That information can be learned through your PGA pro or in a golf instruction manual/video.

First, learn how to hit the shot. Then come back to this chapter and fine-tune your game with these exercises.

HORSE TRAP
2-4 Players

HORSE TRAP is very similar to the other **HORSE GAMES** in previous chapters. This game requires a greenside bunker, two or more players, and lots of imagination.

Before you start, set up a 2-foot diameter tee-circle around the target hole. *(See diagram)*

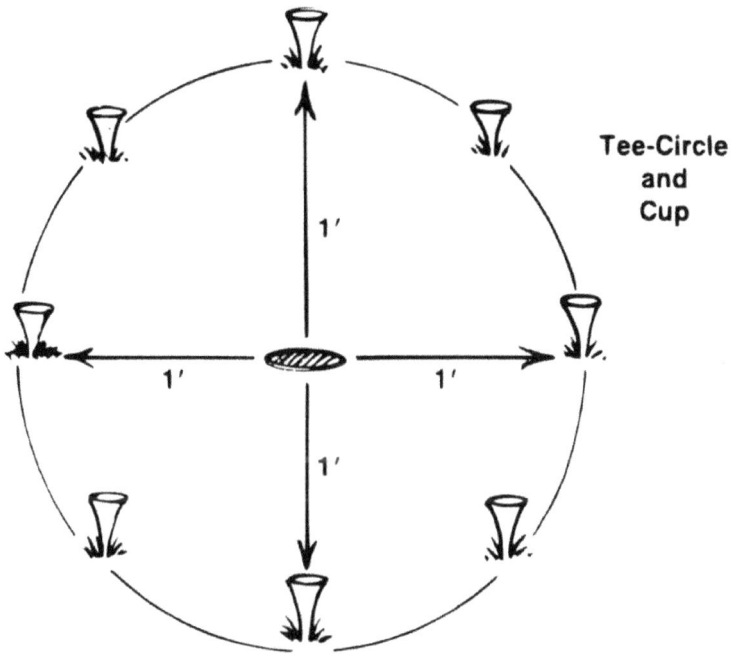

Tee-Circle
and
Cup

To play the game, Player 1 selects a lie in the sand trap. His ball could be buried, uphill, near the back lip, in a footprint, or whatever Player 1 can come up with.

If Player 1 shoots his ball to within the target circle, Player 2 must do the same or receive an **H**. If Player 2 misses, the next player selects a new bunker situation.

But, if the player selecting the lie *misses* the announced target, his turn is skipped and the next player selects a new lie.

Each golfer who accumulates the letters H-O-R-S-E is eliminated, and the last remaining player wins

NOTE— This is a very demanding game, so depending on the skill level of the players, the target diameter can be increased (or decreased).

VARIATION— Instead of the letters **H-O-R-S-E,** try these other golf-related terms:
- **W-E-D-G-E**
- **S-A-N-D-B-O-X**
- **F-R-I-E-D-E-G-G**
- **S-A-N-D-D-U-N-E**
- **S-A-N-D-S-T-O-R-M**
- **Q-U-I-C-K-S-A-N-D**
- **S-A-N-D-C-A-S-T-L-E**

Golf combines two favorite American pastimes—taking a long walk, and hitting things with a stick.

—P.J. O'Rourke

SAND AND PUTT
1-4 Players

Playing a sand shot to within 1-putt range is a great stroke saver, especially when you're trying to save par. **SAND AND PUTT** will give you that extra edge when faced with a par-saving situation. Consistency under pressure is the name of the game.

To start, place four balls in a greenside trap, and all in the same type of lie.

Your goal is to chip each ball onto the green, then sink each with a single putt.

In other words, chip each ball to within 1-putt range.

If you make all four balls with a chip and a putt, place the balls back in the bunker, but this time try a different lie (i.e. buried, in a footprint, almost under the lip, near the back edge of the trap, etc.—be creative).

If you take more than two shots to get up and down, replay the four balls in the same lie.

When playing competitively, use one ball per player and set up each shot in the same lie (i.e. each player chips from a buried lie, or a footprint, etc.).

Play 18 holes—the lowest score wins

SAND TARGET
1-4 Players

When trying to hole out a trap shot, the first question you should ask yourself is, *"where do I want the ball to land?"* As with all **PRESSURE GAMES,** you should *always* pick a target spot no matter what club you use, driver through sand wedge.

Since we're working with the sand wedge here, your target spot will be somewhere on the putting green. *For this game, do not worry about getting the ball close to the hole.*

Your goal is to hit five consecutive shots on the target, and on the fly.

To start, plant four tees on the putting surface, forming a 2-foot square. *(See illustration.)*

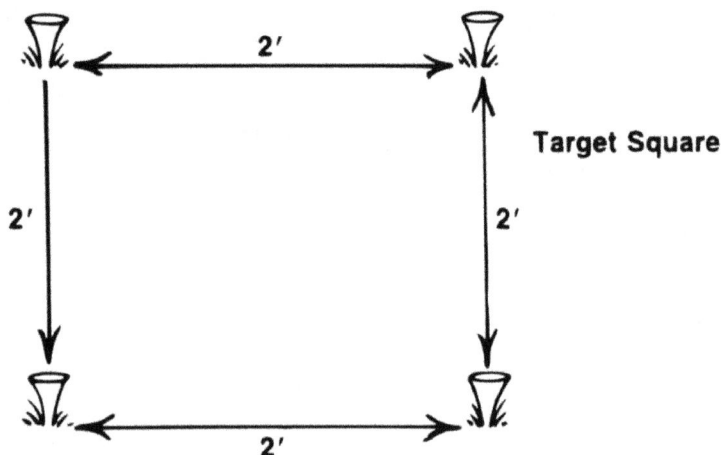

Target Square

Set up this target about 5 yards from the trap. Start with about 10 balls, and try to land your shots inside the square, on the fly.

As you get better, increase your goal to 8, 12, 15, then 20 successful shots in a row. If you miss one, start over.

NOTE— The better you get at this game, the smaller the target should be.

To compete with your friends, try this scoring system:

> Hit target on the fly = **1 point**
>
> Miss target = **2 points**
>
> Ball left in the sand trap = **3 points**

Play 18 holes—low score wins

Relaxation is the key— keep cool under pressure.

—Nancy Lopez

IN A ROW
1-4 Players

IN A ROW, a game you have seen in previous chapters, tests your consistency under pressure. Although best played with two or more friends, the solo version is just as challenging.

The easiest way to set up **IN A ROW** is to plant a circle of tees around the hole you intend to shoot to. Make the circle about 2 feet in diameter. *(See diagram)*

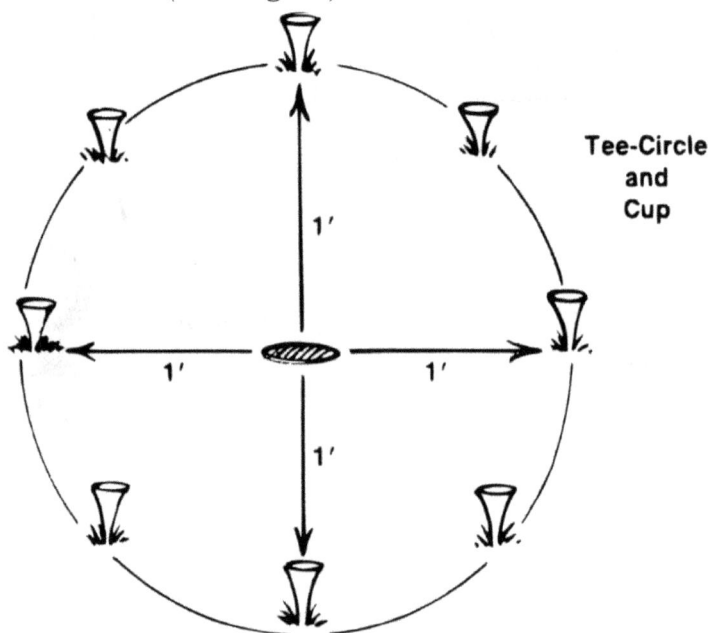

Tee-Circle
and
Cup

If practicing by yourself, hit 10-15 balls from the sand trap, landing as many as you can inside the target circle. If, during a practice session, you put three consecutive shots inside the circle, your next session should require at least four shots in a row.

The objective is to work your way up to 20 consecutive target shots.

When this goal is accomplished, *reduce the size of the target circle.*

If playing against others, Player 1 shoots from the bunker to the target. If he lands inside the circle, he gets 1 point and continues to shoot until he misses. Player 2 then does the same.

The object is to hit the target as many times in a row as you can, collecting 1 point for each success

20 points is a game, but every player should get the same number of turns.

VARIATION— Play from different lies in the trap: in a footprint, ball buried, wet sand, near the edge of the trap.

Also, since each golf course has a different consistency of sand, practice at as many golf courses as you can, and especially where you will compete in the future.

Never let the pressure exceed the pleasure.
—Jack Nicklaus

DON'T GO HOME YET
1 Player

If you want to massively improve your sand game (mentally and physically), play **DON'T GO HOME YET** at least once a day. The game is frustrating, but worth your time.

Put about 10-20 balls in a greenside bunker and start chipping to the cup.

Your goal, before going home, is to hole out three sand shots (but <u>not consecutively</u>).

If you are a beginner at this game, shoot to a larger target. Try setting up a range-ball basket over the cup—*your goal is to hit the basket five times*. After a few successful sessions of this, remove the basket and go for the cup.

VARIATION— Try different lies in the trap (buried, fried-egg, close to the front or back lip, wet or powdery sand, in a footprint, feet above or below the ball).

VARIATION— Go to different courses to try out the different sand consistencies. Not all courses have the same kind of sand that your home course has.

VARIATION— If you are becoming a master with your sand wedge, play this game with your other irons (pitching wedge through 6-iron).

ON THE BEACH VARIATIONS

Just in case the **ON THE BEACH** games are not quite challenging enough, try these variations (some are repeats that appeared in descriptions of the games):

- Go to other golf courses to play from different sand textures. Some courses use light, powdery sand while others use heavy, coarse sand. Try them all for a well-rounded sand game.

- Play from wet sand, hardpan, rocky sand, sand with weeds growing in it, unraked sand.

- Play from different lies: buried, fried-egg, footprint, next to the front or back edge, ball above or below feet, sidehill lies, next to the right or left trap lip.

- Try different irons other than the sand wedge: pitching wedge through 6-iron.

- Extreme conditions— Wind, heat, cold, rain _with no lightning_, snow, sunrise, sunset, noise, talking, traffic sounds, airplanes, barking dogs, loud music.

- Place loose impediments near your ball. These would include natural objects such as twigs, leaves, small stones, pine needles (refer to the current edition of *The Rules of Golf*).

- Chip to various types of greens: wet, dry, fast, slow, sloped, different types of grass.

Create your own variations. You never know what type of situation you might encounter on the course.

8

PRESSURE RULES

LEARNING THE RULES
WITH PRESSURE GAMES

How many golfers really know the *rules of golf?*

I was shocked to find out that many touring professional golfers do not know the rules of their own game. And an even greater percentage of amateur players have no idea what a rule book looks like.

Today, you can have the entire *RULES OF GOLF* on your phone, or you can get an official *USGA RULES OF GOLF* rule book at **WWW.USGA.ORG**. *(USGA = United States Golf Association)*

If you're truly a serious player, explore and join the USGA. Their website is a treasure trove of golf-related instruction, learning the rules, workshops, tournaments, and merchandise.

YouTube is another fantastic place to learn the rules of golf. There are days and days of instruction on just about anything you need to know about golf.

PRESSURE RULES is an innovative approach to understanding, experiencing, and appreciating the 25 rules of this great game.

NOTE— When the first edition of this book came out in 1988, there were 34 rules of golf. But, to streamline the game, AND provide rule modifications for players with disabilities, the USGA now has a list of rules to make the game fair for <u>all</u> to compete.

Knowing the rules can save you strokes, avoid embarrassing situations, and help you win tournaments.

If you play the game, LEARN THE RULES!

You might as well praise a man for not robbing a bank as to praise him for playing by the rules.

—Bobby Jones

LEARNING THE RULES
1-4 Players

LEARNING THE RULES is the only game you will need to understand and use the rules of golf. Not only will you experience situations involving specific rules, you will experience them *under pressure.*

Before you begin, you will need a current copy of the **USGA Rules of Golf.** This is the official booklet put out by the United States Golf Association and contains the rules (and other information) of this fascinating game. You can pick one up at most golf course pro shops, or from the USGA website, **WWW.USGA.ORG.**

To play **LEARNING THE RULES** by yourself, choose one or two of the rules you would like to concentrate on for that practice session. *Know them and understand them before beginning.*

Now, armed with your clubs and rule book, go out to the practice range and *practice the rules*.

To *practice the rules,* put your ball in various situations covered by the rules you are working on. You have four steps to follow:

Step 1 — Identify the situation/what type of problem is your ball in?

Step 2 — What options do you have to correct the problem?

Step 3 — What is the penalty, if any, for each option?

Step 4 — Perform each option.

For example: Today you are going to work on *Rule 16 — Relief from Abnormal Course Conditions,* and the abnormal condition will be ***temporary water.***

First, take the time to read and learn Rule 16 in its entirety. What is an *abnormal course condition?* How is it marked? Where can you drop the ball? What is the penalty?

Now, finding an abnormal condition on a practice range can be a little difficult, so you may have to get creative. Pretend a bare spot on the range tee-area is *temporary water* from a sprinkler system leak. Imagine your drive landed in the middle of the fairway, but stopped on the *temporary water/bare spot.* Now, use the rules to obtain a free drop from that *abnormal condition.*

Your goal is to follow the steps to get out of this problem.

Step 1 — Identify the situation and what rule may apply to this problem.

Step 2 — Looking over the rule, what options do you have to correct this problem? Can you play the ball as it lies? Are you able to take a free drop? Where are you allowed to drop?

Step 3 — What options will result in a penalty? What options can you take to avoid a penalty?

Step 4 — To better learn the rule, **perform each option**, and finish by hitting the ball toward a selected target on the range.

NOTE— Review how to *correctly* drop a ball according to *Rule 14.3 — Dropping Ball in Relief Area.*

Years ago, you dropped a ball over your shoulder and behind you. Today, you hold the ball at knee-height and drop it. Check out the rule before you play.

For each rule you are practicing, try to put your ball in at least *three* different situations that the rule would pertain to. If you are unclear about a rule, ask your PGA professional in the pro shop, or try finding an explanation on YouTube. But your *best option* is accessing the USGA.ORG site.

Another option is doing an Amazon search for books on explaining golf rules. But make sure you get the most current publication; the older books won't have the latest rule updates. Also, do a Google or a YouTube search for *golf rules explained*. A lot of the updated rules are there for you.

NOTE— Make sure any YouTube videos are no more than one or two years old—you want the latest rule updates.

To play **LEARNING THE RULES** with your friends, try the following **PRESSURE GAME:**

Player 1 places a ball in a manner that requires a ruling. Player 2 proceeds through the four steps in solving the problem. If Player 2 makes the correct decisions, he gets to set up a situation for the next player. If a wrong decision/ruling is made, that player receives two penalty strokes and the previous player sets up a new situation for the next player. Any player accumulating six penalty strokes is disqualified, and the last remaining player wins.

NOTE— To keep up-to-date on current rule changes and decisions, read the major golf magazines, do a USGA.ORG or a Google search on *decisions on the rules of golf*, but make sure the decisions are for the current rules.

Trust me, if you want to look like a genius on the course, LEARN AND USE THE RULES

9

PRESSURE PRACTICE

WHAT TO PRACTICE
HOW TO PRACTICE

Knowing *how* to practice is just as important as knowing *what* to practice. In this chapter, you will be guided through a winning practice routine, a pre-game warm-up session, several improvement games, and a great way to plan your next 18-hole attack.

Take some time to try these suggestions. Their purpose is to give you that all-important *edge* over your opponent, and especially in *pressure situations.*

(This box is a brief repeat from the INTRODUCTION)

Again, I am recommending Angela Duckworth's 2016 classic,

GRIT: THE POWER OF PASSION
AND PERSERVERANCE

Read the entire book but memorize *Chapter 7*. Her research on *deliberate practice* and setting a *stretch goal* will enhance your work-focus on the driving range and putting green.

Practice like a winner and you'll play like a winner.

THE WINNER'S ROUTINE

Routines are a valuable part of an outstanding life—just ask any pilot, any surgeon, any military leader, any second-grade teacher, or any successful pro golfer. They, and hundreds of other amazing people, have a routine that is meticulously fine-tuned and religiously followed from the time they wake-up in the morning until they go to bed at night. They know what works and what doesn't, and they use their routine as a catalyst to achieve great things.

One way of making sure your practice session pays off is to follow a set routine. Running out to the range, hitting a bucket of balls, then going to the clubhouse for a beer is a *loser's routine.* If you are truly serious about lowering your handicap, about being fearless on the course, and about *winning,* try the following **WINNER'S ROUTINE:**

Following is a **Pre-Practice Routine** to be done before any practice session. And next, a **Practice Routine** to be followed during the actual practice session.

Pre-Practice Routine

1 — Do some gentle twisting and stretching to loosen the arm, back, and leg muscles.

2 — Gently swing a long iron back and forth, gradually building to a full-force stroke.

3 — Hit five balls with each of the following clubs: pitching wedge, 9-iron, 7-iron, 5-iron, 3-iron, 4-wood, 3-wood, and finishing with the driver.

~Swing smooth and easy — *no power shots~*

NOTE— For the *Practice Routine,* choose whatever three areas of your game need attention (i.e. 5-iron fading approach shots, fairway woods, and left-to-right breaking putts). Then select the three **PRESSURE GAMES** you feel you need to concentrate on:

Sample Practice Routine (3 hours)

Session 1 — (45 minutes) Work on 5-iron fades to a specific target using the **SOLO 7** iron game.
~Break 15 minutes~

Session 2 — (45 minutes) Practice 4-wood shots to a target, playing **IN A ROW** from the **IN THE WOODS** chapter.
~Break 15 minutes~

Session 3 — Play the **PRO SIDE BREAKING** putting game.
~Break 15 minutes~

Session (Optional) — (45 minutes) Review the *USGA Out Of Bounds* rules, then follow the **4-Step** sequence in the **LEARNING THE RULES** chapter.

Session (Optional) — Play **DON'T GO HOME YET** from the **SHORT SHOTS** or **ON THE BEACH** chapters. (limit time to 45 minutes)

A *3-hour session* (three 45-minute sessions with 15-minute breaks), and concentrating on no more than *three different areas,* was found to be the *optimal learning time and sequence* for developing mastery of <u>any</u> subject or skill. Adding an optional session is only allowed after successfully achieving what you set out to do in Sessions 1, 2, and/or 3.

BEFORE YOU PLAY

Before a round of golf, it is best to go through **a *pre-game routine*** to help you warm up and relax.

If you ever attend a PGA tournament, watch the pros warm up on the practice tee. **First**, they stretch and twist to loosen the muscles. **Next**, after swinging a club a few times, they start hitting range balls with several of their clubs. And **last**, they head to the practice green for about 15 minutes of putting.

Their entire routine is short and simple; it loosens the muscles, gets the swing working, and puts the mind in gear for *golf.*

One thing the pre-game routine is *not* is a practice session. One of the worst things you can do is spend your important warm-up time trying to straighten out a slice you've had for nine years. That type of practice is best left for *after* the 18 holes.

Play the game you know—not the game you are desperately trying to build 20 minutes before teeing off.

Right now, all you want to do is warm up those muscles and that brain. The following routine is short, simple, and complete.

The main idea is to reduce those first-tee jitters.

Here is a 45-minute pre-game routine that will prepare you for just about anything:

Pre-Game Routine (45 minutes)

1 — Very Important—Arrive at the course at least an hour before you tee off.

2 — Do some gentle twisting and stretching to loosen the arm, back, and leg muscles.

3 — Gently swing a long iron back and forth, gradually building to a full-force stroke.

4 — Hit five balls with each of the odd or even-numbered clubs. Start with the pitching wedge and work your way up through the woods. Finish with the club you intend to tee off with. (*Save five balls for step 6 below*)

~Swing smooth and easy — *no power shots*~

5 — Using two balls, practice 9 holes of putting. Try to sink every putt, but more important, try to hit the ball *past* the hole—*leave nothing short.*

6 — Immediately before teeing off, make one last stop to the practice range. Using the club you will tee off with, hit five more shots—*smooth and easy.* This will complete the warm-up routine and get you ready for that all-important first drive.

Don't be too proud to take lessons—
I'm not.   *Jack Nicklaus*

ONE CLUB ROUND
1-4 Players

Toward the end of the day, when there are not many golfers on the course, take some balls and *one* of your clubs and play 9 holes.

Playing with a single club, and usually an iron, can do wonders for your game. Not only will you build confidence with that particular club, you will be amazed at how, creatively, certain situations can be handled.

For example, how are you going to play from a greenside bunker with a 5-iron? Or, what route do you take over a small lake when all you have is a wedge?

Problems like these will need your best creative solutions. And just think of the possibilities when you get to use all 14 clubs.

If you want to compete with your friends, play a one-club tournament with each golfer selecting their own weapon.

NOTE— I've seen the pros play this game, and their club-of-choice is the 4-iron.

You swing your best when you have the fewest things to think about.

—*Bobby Jones*

FOUR CLUB ROUND
1-4 Players

This game is played just like **ONE CLUB ROUND**. The difference is you may use *four clubs* instead of one. Any four clubs will do, but to get the most from this game, select *a wood, an iron, a wedge, and a putter.*

If you are playing by yourself, use the clubs you have the most difficulty with. Playing these clubs through 9 holes of golf will help you become more comfortable with them. You are allowed 14 clubs in your bag—learn to use them all.

To play against your partners, each golfer selects four clubs. Play 9 or 18 holes, and score as you normally would. To restrict club selection, require each player to bring *a wood, an iron, a wedge, and a putter.* This rule is unnecessary, but it adds some challenge to the game.

VARIATION— Try tournaments using 2, 3, 5, or 6 clubs. You are limited only by your imagination.

Professional golf is the only sport where if you win 20% of the time, you're the best.

—Jack Nicklaus

ONE CLUB, ONE SHOT
1-4 Players

ONE CLUB, ONE SHOT is a great way to finish a session on the driving range. You might consider this a *final test* of your target-striking ability, which you may have been practicing for the past hour or two.

To set up, place your last 13 range balls to the side. Next, lay out, on the ground, your 13 clubs (putter excluded).

Starting with any club you wish and one ball, select an appropriate target and shoot for it. If you hit the target, great—if you miss, tough.

ONE CLUB, ONE SHOT is just like playing on the golf course—*you only get one chance.* After shooting your one ball, put the club in the bag and select another club, then shoot another ball.

NOTE— After going through your 13 clubs and balls, reflect back on the amount of success you had. What clubs were you most comfortable with? What clubs did you feel less confident with? During the next practice session, work on those *difficult* clubs, and eventually make them your favorites.

To play **ONE CLUB, ONE SHOT** competitively, each player should, first, set up as described above—13 clubs, 13 balls. To start the game, a club and target are agreed upon. For instance, each player must shoot a 6-iron to the 150-yard marker. Be sure to determine how large of a landing area surrounds each target.

Score as outlined below:

> Hitting the target = **1 point**
> Missing the target = **2 points**
> Short of target = **3 points**

Lowest score after 13 shots wins

VARIATION— Instead of 13 balls, try 26 or 39. Go through each of the 13 clubs before repeating.

VARIATION— See the end of the chapters **MADE OF IRON, IN THE WOODS, DRIVE,** and **ON THE BEACH** for variations on each club group.

Success depends almost entirely on how effectively you learn to manage the game's two ultimate adversaries— the course and yourself.

—Jack Nicklaus

OFFICE GOLF
1-4 Players

If many of your co-workers play golf, here is a little office game that could turn into a grand scale tournament. During your lunch break, set up a 9-hole putting course in a vacant portion of the office. Use nine objects as targets (i.e. coffee cups, paper clip boxes, rolls of tape). Each hole should be a par 2. But, if you wish to include a par 3 hole, make it a dogleg. Play as you would a regular round of golf with the lowest score winning.

If your fellow workers are competitive players, set up a 4-day, 36-hole tournament. Use the office copier to run off some rules and scorecards, set up a leaderboard, and collect a $10.00 entry fee from each participant. The entry fees are used as prize money for the first, second, and third place winners.

Here are some rules you may want to consider:

> ✓ Free drop from wires
>
> ✓ Under a desk is out-of-bounds
>
> ✓ Ball against a wall or desk leg may be moved 4 inches from obstruction—no penalty
>
> ✓ Hitting any part of the target hole is considered *sinking the putt*
>
> ✓ Loose impediments such as paper clips, rubber bands, or dropped pencils may be removed
>
> ✓ Conduct play according to the USGA Rules of Golf (as much as you can)

These types of tournaments are great for boosting office morale. After four hours of sales meetings, phone calls, and customer complaints, it is always nice to have a little "play time."

IDEA— If *you* are the boss, boost morale by offering a free *lunch with the boss* for the tournament winner.

IDEA— Organize an office putting team and challenge other offices in the building.

No matter how good you are, you can always get better—and that's the exciting part.

—Gary Player

INDOOR PUTTING
1-4 Players

When the weather is not cooperating or the course is closed for the day, try playing 18 holes of **INDOOR PUTTING.**

Set up a 9 or 18-hole putting course through the living room, dining room, hallway, and bedrooms. As targets, use food cans, baby toys, plastic cups, or whatever is available.

Each hole should be a par 2, straight away with no doglegs.

Par for 18 holes is 36 putts. If you shoot *over par* for the 18 holes, start over at hole number one.

Also, keep a record chart of your scores and use your *lowest score* as a goal for each time you play.

When playing with the family, the lowest score wins (and the losers do the dishes).

NOTE— If you are putting on carpet, beware of the *grain* of the fibers. Notice which way the longer putts break, then allow for this *grain-induced* influence.

VARIATION— If the space is tiny, you may need to set up some dogleg holes. Limit dogleg pars to 3 putts.

VARIATION—If you feel you are ready for more of a challenge, set up your course for par 1 short holes, or longer holes with higher pars. Be creative with this game.

INDOOR CHIPPING
1-4 Players

As with **INDOOR PUTTING,** when the weather is not ideal, or the course is closed, try playing **INDOOR CHIPPING.**

Now, before you start thinking of all the damage that might happen when hitting golf balls inside the house, let me explain.

I first mentioned my high school golf coach, Don O'Hare, in the putting chapter. This was another idea of his that I've used for 50+ years. Since the springtime weather in Colorado wasn't always perfect for our golf team going to the course for some after-school practice, we used the gym to hit balls.

The one difference is, we used plastic practice balls (the ones with the holes) to hit full-swing shots from one end of the gym to the other.

Now, if you've ever hit a plastic practice ball, it doesn't feel like anything, so we stuffed those balls with torn up cotton rags. This gave the balls a little weight, so it felt like you were really *hitting* something. I carried this over to chipping balls in my parents' basement game room. It worked great!

NOTE— If you're going to practice chipping around a *carpeted* house, pick up a 2' x 3' remnant carpet sample or door mat to hit off of. Taking a divot out of your wall-to-wall could cause problems. Trust me, I know from experience—sorry, Mom.

Remnants and door mats can be found at Walmart, Home Depot, a carpet outlet, or a local thrift store. Just make sure it's not too thin.

To start, stuff about a dozen plastic balls with some rag material (stuff them using a pencil). Then set up a few areas in the living room, dining room, hallway, or bedrooms that will work for small chipping targets.

Maybe use some pillows, some folded blankets, books, sheets of newspaper, or a laundry basket padded with towels.

Set up a small 9-hole course throughout the house and *chip* to these targets. Remember, chipping is not a full-swing stroke, and be sure to *use your carpet remnant.*

If playing by yourself, just chip five balls to land on a target. If you land all five on the target, increase the distance or increase the number of balls. If you miss, start over.

Your goal is to land the ball, on the fly, on the target.

When playing with family or friends, use the following scoring system:

Hitting the target = **1 point**
Missing the target = **2 points**
Short of target = **3 points**

Lowest score after 18 shots wins

NOTE— Stuffed plastic balls are still a hazard to others and to fragile property, so don't be too aggressive with your swing.

VARIATION— You don't necessarily need to set up a 9-hole course around the house. Hitting to a single target still works for improving your short game.

INDOOR HIT AND RUN
1-4 Players

As with **INDOOR CHIPPING,** when the weather is not ideal, or the course is closed, try playing **INDOOR HIT AND RUN.**

First, review the previous game, **INDOOR CHIPPING,** to prepare your practice tools, including the carpet remnant.

To start, stuff about a dozen plastic balls with some rag material (stuff them using a pencil). Then set up a few areas in the living room, dining room, hallway, or bedrooms that will work for hit-and-run targets. Use items that can work as a backstop for a rolling ball: books, cardboard boxes, couch cushions, large toys, etc.

Give yourself about 20 feet of floor space for these hit-and-run shots, and make sure the floor/carpeting works for rolling balls; shag carpet will not work very well.

What you do here is, using a hit-and-run club like a 5 or 7-iron, chip to your target and hit it on the roll, not on the fly. Pretend the target is the hole.

If playing by yourself, just hit five balls to run to a target. If you run all five to the target, increase the distance or increase the number of balls. If you miss, start over.

Your goal is to run/roll the ball to the target.

When playing with family or friends, use the following scoring system:

Hitting the target = **1 point**

Missing the target = **2 points**

Short of the target = **3 points**

Lowest score after 18 shots wins

NOTE— Stuffed plastic balls are still a hazard to others and to fragile property, so don't be too aggressive with your swing.

VARIATION— Set up a small, flat obstacle to hit over (some books, magazines, newspaper, etc.) and imagine you are hitting over a small sand trap or some thick grass.

Pressure comes from feeling you have something to lose. Play freely and aggressively.

—Phil Mickelson

AUTOMATIC RETURN
1-4 Players

If you have one of those 12-inch wide automatic ball returners gathering dust in the garage, let's *putt* it to good use.

Since the hole on a putting green is 4 ¼ inches wide and not 12 inches, we need to narrow our target. With some white typewriter correction fluid, or a small piece of bright tape, put a small dot on the center entry ramp of the ball returner.

Next, place the device on the floor and set up 10 dimes in a straight line from the returner, each one foot apart. *(See diagram)*

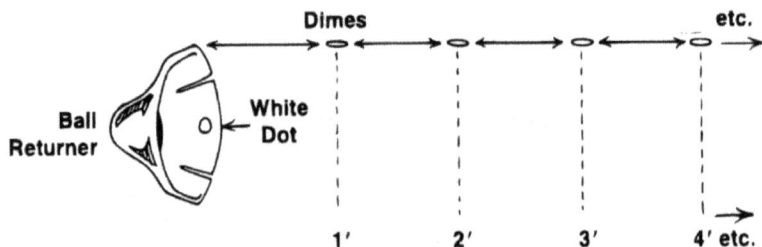

Starting at the 1-foot dime line and using a single ball, hit 10 straight putts *over the white dot* and into the ball returner.

Next, do the same from the 2-foot dime and eventually working your way to 10 feet without missing the little white target. If you miss, move one dime closer and start over.

To compete with your friends, try the following game:

> ➢ Starting at the 1-foot mark, each player putts two times in a row.
>
> Going over the dot = **1 point**
> Missing the dot = **2 points**
> Missing the ball returner = **3 points**
>
> ➢ Write down the scores after each round.
>
> ➢ After all players have putted two balls, move to the 2-foot mark, and repeat the process.
>
> ➢ Total the scores after everyone has putted from the 10-foot dime.

Low score wins

NOTE— If you are putting on carpet, beware of the *grain* of the fibers. Notice which way the longer putts break, then allow for this *grain-induced* influence.

Pressure can make you swing too fast and lose control. Swing easy and keep tempo.

Ernie Els

GAME PLAN

One cause of pressure that few golfers are aware of is not knowing *where* on the fairway or green to place the ball. What is needed here is a hole-by-hole **GAME PLAN.**

This is basically a strategy to play to your strengths and to avoid unnecessary risks. This plan should be set up according to your skill-level while making adjustments for weather conditions, course layout, and your goals for that particular round.

A **GAME PLAN** can be developed by answering these two basic questions:

> 1 – Where, *on the fairway*, do I want to place my drive?
>
> 2 – Where, *on the green*, will my approach shot leave me the easiest putt?

If you play one course almost exclusively, it would be to your advantage to draw up a strategy for each hole. Knowing in advance *where* to hit the ball relieves a fair amount of nervous pressure, and will certainly eliminate wasted strokes.

The best way to begin is to take a small notebook out on the course and make a sketch of each hole. Include sand and water hazards, trees, bushes, out-of-bounds, the 150-yard markers, and the general slope of each green.

Your rough sketch might look like this:

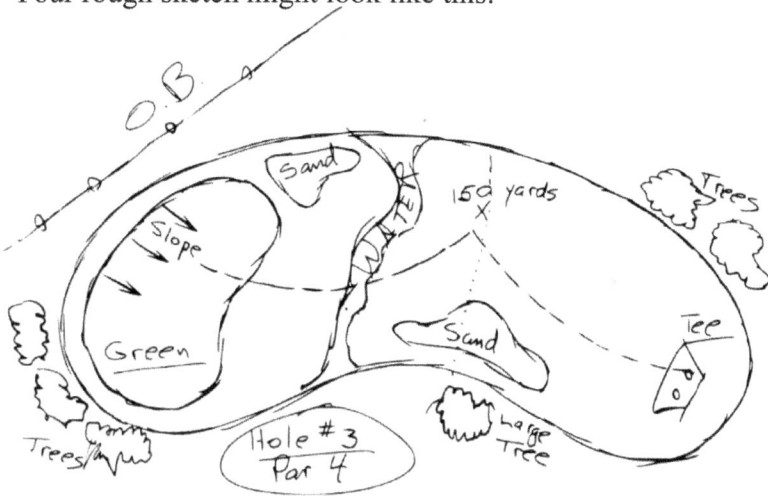

After sketching the hole, stand at the back of the green and face the fairway. From here, you can easily determine the best target areas you want to hit with your drive and approach shot.

Mark these areas on your drawing with an "**X**."

After all 18 holes have been sketched out and all target areas have been determined, take your notebook home and *neatly* re-draw each hole.

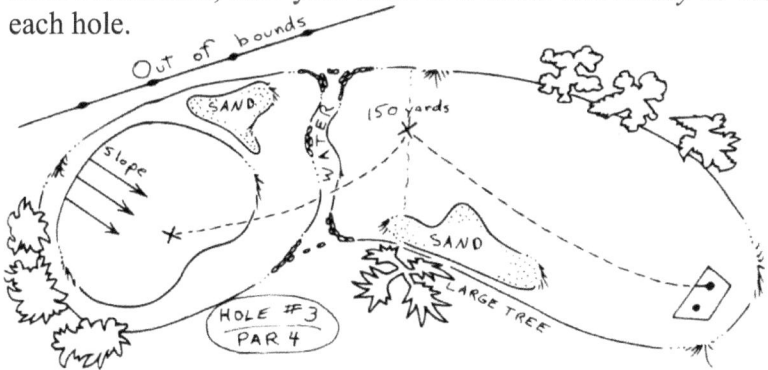

Later, if you really want to get into detail, measure yardages from certain landmarks to the front edge of the green, and write these on your diagrams. Basically, what you will end up with is a *yardage book* much like the professional golfers use.

A professional *yardage book* contains detailed information about each hole on the golf course. Included in these booklets are hazards, out-of-bounds, the slope of the greens, and other pertinent info to assist golfers in managing the course and developing a winning strategy.

To get the most from your **GAME PLAN,** you need to study it. And the most effective way to study it is to follow this 3-step process for each hole:

---

1 – Study the drawing. Notice the placement of trees, bunkers, target areas, and slope of the green.

2 – Close your eyes and relax. Visualize yourself hitting the ball to each target area. Jack Nicklaus called this "Watching the movie." Each shot is perfect—no pressure.

3 – After you have mentally played all 18 holes, repeat steps 1 and 2 for one more flawless practice round.

This 3-step plan is an extremely effective tool in preparing you for a great round of golf. Use it at least 30 minutes before heading out to the course.

NOTE— Here's a little background on *yardage books*:

Yardage books have been around since the 1960s. Pro golfer and former PGA Tour commissioner Deane Beman is credited with starting this trend, later sharing it with Arnold Palmer and Jack Nicklaus. Arnie and Jack both had homemade yardage books to help them navigate the courses they competed on. Each hole was drawn out with all the trees, bushes, hazards, greens, and other pertinent information.

Yardage books were commercialized by former caddie Mark Long. Starting in 1992, he sold these tiny booklets at all the professional tournaments, and *every* pro would purchase one before playing. This practice continues today.

I met Mark at the Phoenix Open and bought one of his first yardage books for around $5; today, they're about $40.

Currently, there are probably a dozen or more apps that can help you make yardage books for just about any course you play.

If you want to explore more about yardage books and learn how to make your own, do a Google search for *golf yardage books, Mark Long yardage books, how to make a golf yardage book, caddies and yardage books,* or whatever interests you about the subject. There are also several Amazon books on the subject.

And, if you're a visual learner, there are more YouTube videos than you will ever want to see about yardage books and course management. Check them out.

My advice is to make your own yardage book. You know your course; you know the best target areas to hit the ball; you know where the obstacles and hazards are, *and you know your own game.* First, learn *how* to make one, then make your own customized book.

PRESSURE GAMES FOR GOLF

ABOUT THE AUTHOR

George Haughton is a teacher, writer, and longtime student of the game of golf. After years of observing how golfers practice and perform under pressure, he developed the practice games featured in this book to help players build mental toughness and confidence on the course.

His work focuses on practical training methods that transform ordinary practice sessions into meaningful preparation for competition.

A NOTE FROM THE AUTHOR

Thank you for reading Pressure Games For Golf.

My hope is that these games make your practice sessions more focused, competitive, and enjoyable. Golf is a game that rewards discipline, patience, and preparation. When you learn to practice under pressure, the course begins to feel familiar rather than intimidating.

Use these games regularly. Share them with your friends, teammates, and coaches. And, modify them if needed.

The goal isn't perfection—it's improvement.

Most of all, remember that golf is meant to be played and enjoyed. The more purpose you bring to your practice, the more confidence you'll bring to the course.

INDEX OF
PRESSURE GAMES

Thanks for purchasing
PRESSURE GAMES FOR GOLF

If you enjoyed this book, please leave a review on Amazon to let other golfers know how to also improve *their* game.

Again, thanks,
George Haughton